Fine-Tuning LLM

Advanced Techniques for Optimizing AI Performance with PyTorch and Hugging Face

©

Written By
Camila Jones

Copyright

Table of Content

Chapter 1: Introduction to Fine-Tuning LLMs

1.1 The Evolution of Large Language Models

The development of large language models (LLMs) represents a journey spanning several decades. From early rule-based systems and statistical models to today's deep learning architectures, each step has built upon previous breakthroughs to enable computers to understand and generate human language with increasing sophistication.

Early Beginnings

Before the advent of deep learning, natural language processing (NLP) relied on rule-based systems and statistical models. Early methods involved manually coded grammar rules and simple statistical approaches such as n-gram models. An **n-gram model** predicts the next word in a sequence based on the previous *n-1* words. Although these models were useful for certain tasks, they had major limitations:

- **Context Limitation:** They could only consider a fixed number of previous words.
- **Data Sparsity:** As the value of *n* increased, the required data to capture all possible word sequences grew exponentially.
- **Lack of Semantics:** They could not capture the deeper meaning or context of language.

The Neural Network Era

The introduction of neural networks marked a turning point. Recurrent Neural Networks (RNNs) and later Long Short-Term Memory networks (LSTMs) were designed to process sequences of data, making them a natural fit for language tasks. These models were able to maintain information across longer sequences, addressing some limitations of n-gram models. However, they still faced challenges such as:

- **Vanishing Gradients:** Difficulty in learning long-range dependencies in sequences.
- **Computational Bottlenecks:** Slow training times and difficulty in parallel processing.

The Transformer Revolution

In 2017, the publication of the paper "Attention Is All You Need" introduced the **Transformer** architecture. Transformers use self-attention mechanisms to weigh the importance of different words in a sentence, regardless of their position. This approach overcame many limitations of previous models by:

- **Handling Long-Range Dependencies:** The self-attention mechanism allows the model to focus on relevant parts of the input regardless of distance.
- **Parallelization:** Unlike RNNs and LSTMs, Transformers allow for more efficient training on modern hardware, significantly reducing training times.

The Transformer architecture paved the way for the creation of models that are both larger and more capable. Two key models that emerged from this era include:

- **BERT (Bidirectional Encoder Representations from Transformers):** Introduced by Google, BERT leverages a bidirectional approach to understand context from both left and right of each word.
- **GPT (Generative Pre-trained Transformer):** Developed by OpenAI, GPT models focus on generating coherent and contextually appropriate text, and have evolved through several iterations (GPT-2, GPT-3, and beyond).

Milestones in the Evolution of LLMs

Below is a timeline table summarizing the key milestones in the evolution of language models:

Time Period	Model/Approach	Key Contributions
1950s - 1980s	Rule-Based and Statistical Models	Early work in NLP using hand-crafted rules and n-gram statistics.
1990s - Early 2000s	N-gram Models	Introduced statistical methods for predicting language sequences.

2000s	Recurrent Neural Networks (RNNs)	Applied neural networks to sequence processing with limited context.
Late 2000s - 2010s	LSTM and GRU Models	Improved handling of long-range dependencies in text.
2017	Transformer Architecture	Introduced self-attention and parallel processing capabilities.
2018	BERT	Advanced understanding of bidirectional context in language.
2019 - Present	GPT Series (GPT-2, GPT-3, etc.)	Focused on generating high-quality, coherent text using transformers.
2020s	Fine-Tuned LLMs and Multimodal Models	Integration of fine-tuning methods and additional modalities (e.g., images, speech).

Table 1.1: Timeline of the Evolution of Large Language Models

Code Example: Exploring a Pre-Trained LLM

To give you a hands-on taste of working with modern LLMs, here's a simple example using the Hugging Face Transformers library. This code demonstrates how to load a pre-trained GPT-2 model and generate text:

python

```python
# Import the pipeline function from the transformers library

from transformers import pipeline


# Create a text generation pipeline using the GPT-2 model

generator = pipeline("text-generation", model="gpt2")


# Generate text based on a given prompt

prompt = "The evolution of language models has been remarkable because"

generated_text = generator(prompt, max_length=100,
num_return_sequences=1)


# Print the generated text

print("Generated Text:")

print(generated_text[0]['generated_text'])
```

Explanation:

1. **Importing Pipeline:** The pipeline function simplifies the process of using pre-trained models for various tasks. Here, it is used for text generation.
2. **Loading the Model:** The model "gpt2" is loaded from the Hugging Face model hub.
3. **Text Generation:** The prompt is passed to the model, which then generates a continuation of the text. Parameters such as max_length control the length of the output.
4. **Output:** The generated text is printed, showcasing how GPT-2 extends the prompt based on its training data.

The evolution of large language models is a story of gradual improvement and revolutionary breakthroughs. From the early days of rule-based systems and statistical models to the sophisticated architectures of Transformers, each innovation has contributed to making models that are more capable, efficient, and context-aware. This journey has laid the foundation for modern applications in NLP, setting the stage for further advances in fine-tuning techniques and domain-specific adaptations, which will be explored in the subsequent chapters.

This detailed look at the evolution of LLMs provides the necessary background to understand why fine-tuning has become such a critical step in harnessing the power of these models. As we move forward, we'll build on this knowledge to explore how fine-tuning techniques can be applied to optimize AI performance using tools like PyTorch and Hugging Face.

1.2 The Importance of Fine-Tuning in AI

Fine-tuning plays a critical role in modern AI by bridging the gap between general-purpose pre-trained models and specialized applications. While large language models (LLMs) are trained on vast amounts of diverse data, this pre-training process is inherently generic. Fine-tuning refines these models, allowing them to perform exceptionally well on specific tasks or within particular domains. Below, we explore the reasons why fine-tuning is so important and how it benefits AI systems.

Pre-trained models have learned a wide variety of language patterns, facts, and general knowledge. However, when it comes to domain-specific tasks—such as legal document analysis, medical diagnosis, or technical support—these general models may lack the specialized knowledge required. Fine-tuning adapts the model to:

- **Improve Accuracy:** By exposing the model to domain-specific data, fine-tuning helps it learn nuances and terminology that are unique to a particular field.
- **Increase Relevance:** The model becomes more context-aware, making its responses and predictions more pertinent to the task at hand.

For example, consider a legal chatbot that needs to interpret legal documents accurately. A generic LLM might miss subtle legal terms or fail to understand context-specific language. Fine-tuning on a curated legal dataset can greatly enhance its performance.

Training large models from scratch is both computationally expensive and time-consuming. Fine-tuning offers a practical alternative by leveraging the robust general knowledge of pre-trained models and adapting them to new tasks with relatively small, specialized datasets. This approach:

- **Saves Resources:** Requires less computational power and time than training from scratch.
- **Accelerates Deployment:** Allows faster iteration and deployment of models tailored to specific needs.

One of the strengths of fine-tuning is its flexibility. Organizations can take a single pre-trained model and customize it for a variety of applications without needing to maintain separate, large-scale training pipelines for each use case. Fine-tuning enables:

- **Multi-Domain Adaptation:** A single model can be fine-tuned to handle various specialized tasks with minimal adjustments.
- **Continuous Improvement:** Models can be periodically updated with new data, ensuring that they remain current and effective in rapidly evolving domains.

Pre-trained models may inherit biases present in the large, diverse datasets used during their initial training. Fine-tuning provides an opportunity to address these issues:

- **Bias Reduction:** By carefully selecting and curating the fine-tuning dataset, developers can help mitigate biases and ensure that the model behaves more fairly and responsibly.
- **Ethical AI Practices:** Fine-tuning allows for the integration of ethical guidelines, ensuring that the AI's responses are aligned with social and professional standards.

Fine-tuned models have demonstrated significant improvements in practical applications. Here is a table summarizing the key benefits of fine-tuning:

Aspect	General Pre-Trained Model	Fine-Tuned Model
Domain Relevance	Broad and generic understanding	Specific, nuanced comprehension of domain-specific language
Accuracy	May miss specialized details or context	Higher accuracy on targeted tasks

Resource Efficiency	Requires extensive training from scratch for high performance	Cost-effective adaptation with less data and computational resources
Bias and Fairness	Potentially inherits biases from large-scale, heterogeneous data	Opportunity to correct biases through curated, ethical datasets
Customization	One-size-fits-all approach	Tailored to the unique needs and challenges of specific industries

Table 1.2: Comparison of General Pre-Trained Models vs. Fine-Tuned Models

Below is a simplified code example using the Hugging Face Transformers library to fine-tune a pre-trained model on a custom dataset. In this example, we assume you have a dataset in a CSV file with columns "text" and "label" for a text classification task.

python

```python
import pandas as pd

from sklearn.model_selection import train_test_split

from transformers import AutoTokenizer, AutoModelForSequenceClassification, Trainer, TrainingArguments

from datasets import Dataset


# Load your dataset
```

```python
df = pd.read_csv("custom_dataset.csv")

# Split the dataset into training and validation sets

train_df, val_df = train_test_split(df, test_size=0.2, random_state=42)


# Convert pandas DataFrame to Hugging Face Dataset

train_dataset = Dataset.from_pandas(train_df)

val_dataset = Dataset.from_pandas(val_df)


# Load the tokenizer and model (for example, using a BERT variant)

model_name = "bert-base-uncased"

tokenizer = AutoTokenizer.from_pretrained(model_name)

model =
AutoModelForSequenceClassification.from_pretrained(model_name,
num_labels=2)


# Tokenize the dataset

def tokenize_function(examples):

    return tokenizer(examples["text"], padding="max_length",
truncation=True)


train_dataset = train_dataset.map(tokenize_function, batched=True)

val_dataset = val_dataset.map(tokenize_function, batched=True)


# Define training arguments

training_args = TrainingArguments(
```

```python
    output_dir="./results",

    evaluation_strategy="epoch",

    learning_rate=2e-5,

    per_device_train_batch_size=16,

    per_device_eval_batch_size=16,

    num_train_epochs=3,

    weight_decay=0.01,

)


# Initialize Trainer
trainer = Trainer(

    model=model,

    args=training_args,

    train_dataset=train_dataset,

    eval_dataset=val_dataset,

)


# Start fine-tuning
trainer.train()
```

Explanation:

1. **Data Loading and Preparation:**
   The code reads a CSV file into a pandas DataFrame, then splits the data into
   training and validation sets. The DataFrame is converted into a Hugging Face
   Dataset for compatibility.

2. **Tokenizer and Model Setup:**
    We load a pre-trained BERT model and its tokenizer. The model is configured for sequence classification with a specified number of labels.
3. **Tokenization:**
    A helper function tokenizes the text data, ensuring all inputs are padded and truncated to a consistent length.
4. **Training Arguments:**
    The training parameters are defined, including batch sizes, learning rate, number of epochs, and evaluation strategy.
5. **Trainer Initialization and Training:**
    The Trainer object from Hugging Face orchestrates the training process, fine-tuning the model on the custom dataset.

Fine-tuning is a cornerstone of modern AI development. It transforms a broadly knowledgeable pre-trained model into a finely honed tool, capable of addressing specific tasks with greater accuracy, efficiency, and ethical consideration. By adapting the model to specialized data, fine-tuning not only improves performance but also ensures that AI systems are better aligned with real-world needs and professional standards. This foundational step in AI development sets the stage for more advanced techniques, which we will explore in the following chapters.

1.3 Overview of PyTorch and Hugging Face Ecosystems

In recent years, the PyTorch and Hugging Face ecosystems have emerged as two of the most influential frameworks in the field of natural language processing (NLP) and deep learning. Their combined strengths provide developers and researchers with powerful tools for building, training, and deploying state-of-the-art models, including fine-tuned large language models (LLMs). This section provides an in-depth overview of both ecosystems, explaining their core components, features, and how they integrate to create an accessible and robust environment for AI development.

PyTorch: A Deep Learning Framework

PyTorch is an open-source deep learning library developed by Facebook's AI Research lab. It is widely appreciated for its dynamic computation graph, which allows for flexibility during model development and debugging. Here are some key aspects of the PyTorch ecosystem:

- **Dynamic Computation Graphs:**
  Unlike static computation graph frameworks, PyTorch builds graphs on the fly. This means that changes in the graph (such as those made during debugging or variable sequence lengths) are handled naturally, making it ideal for research and development.
- **Tensor Operations and Autograd:**
  PyTorch provides a robust tensor library similar to NumPy, with additional support for GPU acceleration. Its automatic differentiation system, known as *Autograd*, simplifies the process of computing gradients, a critical aspect of training neural networks.
- **Modular and Intuitive API:**
  PyTorch's modules and layers can be easily composed to create complex architectures. This modularity makes it simple to implement custom models and experiment with novel ideas.
- **Community and Extensions:**
  With a large and active community, PyTorch benefits from a wealth of tutorials, third-party libraries, and integrations. Frameworks like **TorchVision**, **TorchText**, and **PyTorch Lightning** further extend its capabilities for image processing, NLP, and organizing training loops, respectively.

Below is a simple code example demonstrating the use of PyTorch for creating and training a basic neural network:

python

```python
import torch

import torch.nn as nn

import torch.optim as optim


# Define a simple neural network
class SimpleNN(nn.Module):
    def __init__(self, input_size, hidden_size, output_size):
        super(SimpleNN, self).__init__()
        self.fc1 = nn.Linear(input_size, hidden_size)
```

```python
        self.relu = nn.ReLU()

        self.fc2 = nn.Linear(hidden_size, output_size)


    def forward(self, x):

        x = self.fc1(x)

        x = self.relu(x)

        x = self.fc2(x)

        return x


# Create a model instance

model = SimpleNN(input_size=10, hidden_size=5, output_size=1)


# Define a loss function and an optimizer

criterion = nn.MSELoss()

optimizer = optim.Adam(model.parameters(), lr=0.001)


# Dummy input and target tensors

inputs = torch.randn(16, 10)  # batch of 16 samples, 10 features each

targets = torch.randn(16, 1)


# Training loop (one epoch)

for epoch in range(1):

    optimizer.zero_grad()      # Clear gradients
```

```
outputs = model(inputs)      # Forward pass

loss = criterion(outputs, targets)  # Compute loss

loss.backward()              # Backward pass (compute gradients)

optimizer.step()             # Update model parameters

print(f"Epoch [{epoch+1}], Loss: {loss.item():.4f}")
```

Explanation:

- **Model Definition:**
  We define a simple feed-forward neural network with one hidden layer using the nn.Module class.
- **Loss and Optimizer:**
  The Mean Squared Error (MSE) loss is used for regression, and the Adam optimizer is employed for parameter updates.
- **Training Loop:**
  The training loop demonstrates a single epoch where gradients are computed and updated, highlighting the dynamic and intuitive nature of PyTorch.

Hugging Face: Democratizing NLP with Pre-Trained Models

Hugging Face is an AI company and open-source community that has significantly advanced the field of NLP. Its ecosystem revolves around the **Transformers** library, which provides a unified interface for thousands of pre-trained models, including BERT, GPT, T5, and more.

- **Transformers Library:**
  This library makes it easy to load, fine-tune, and deploy transformer-based models. It abstracts the complexity of model architectures and training routines, enabling developers to focus on application-specific tasks.
- **Datasets and Tokenizers:**
  Hugging Face offers dedicated libraries like **Datasets** and **Tokenizers**.
  - **Datasets:** Provides access to a wide range of datasets, along with tools for efficient data processing and handling.

- ○ **Tokenizers:** Optimized for speed and efficiency, the Tokenizers library converts raw text into model-readable tokens while handling various languages and encoding schemes.
- **Model Hub:**
  The Hugging Face Model Hub is a central repository where developers can share and download pre-trained models. It fosters collaboration and accelerates the adoption of state-of-the-art techniques.
- **Community and Documentation:**
  Hugging Face is known for its vibrant community and comprehensive documentation. The ecosystem encourages contributions from researchers and practitioners worldwide, ensuring that the tools remain up-to-date with the latest advances.

Below is a simple code example that demonstrates how to load a pre-trained model for text classification using the Hugging Face Transformers library:

python

```python
from transformers import AutoTokenizer,
AutoModelForSequenceClassification, pipeline


# Specify the pre-trained model to use

model_name = "distilbert-base-uncased-finetuned-sst-2-english"


# Load the tokenizer and model from the Hugging Face Hub

tokenizer = AutoTokenizer.from_pretrained(model_name)

model =
AutoModelForSequenceClassification.from_pretrained(model_name)


# Create a pipeline for sentiment analysis

sentiment_analyzer = pipeline("sentiment-analysis", model=model,
tokenizer=tokenizer)
```

```
# Test the pipeline with a sample input

sample_text = "I love using Hugging Face and PyTorch for my projects!"

result = sentiment_analyzer(sample_text)


print("Sentiment Analysis Result:")

print(result)
```

Explanation:

- **Model Loading:**
  The pre-trained model "distilbert-base-uncased-finetuned-sst-2-english" is loaded along with its tokenizer. This model is fine-tuned for sentiment analysis.
- **Pipeline Creation:**
  The pipeline function creates a high-level abstraction for performing sentiment analysis with a single call.
- **Inference:**
  The sample text is processed through the pipeline, and the output shows the sentiment prediction along with a confidence score.

Integrating PyTorch and Hugging Face

The seamless integration between PyTorch and Hugging Face is one of the key strengths of the combined ecosystem. Hugging Face models are built on PyTorch (and sometimes TensorFlow), allowing users to leverage PyTorch's dynamic computation and extensive community resources while benefiting from Hugging Face's state-of-the-art pre-trained models and tools.

Below is a table summarizing the strengths of each ecosystem:

Feature	PyTorch	Hugging Face

Core Functionality	Deep learning framework with dynamic computation graphs	Library for NLP models, datasets, and tokenizers
Model Development	Flexible, custom neural network architectures	Access to thousands of pre-trained models
Ease of Use	Intuitive and Pythonic API	High-level pipelines and unified interfaces
Community and Support	Large, active community with extensive tutorials	Vibrant open-source community and comprehensive documentation
Deployment	Integration with various deployment platforms and GPU support	Model Hub for sharing and deploying models easily
Customization	Highly customizable model building and training routines	Fine-tuning and transfer learning capabilities for various tasks

Table 1.3: Comparative Overview of PyTorch and Hugging Face Ecosystems

The PyTorch and Hugging Face ecosystems together form a powerful toolkit for anyone involved in AI and NLP. PyTorch provides the low-level control and flexibility required for developing custom neural network architectures and training routines, while Hugging Face offers high-level abstractions, pre-trained models, and tools that simplify the process of working with language models. By leveraging these ecosystems, developers and researchers can accelerate innovation, reduce development time, and achieve state-of-the-art performance in various AI applications.

This comprehensive overview sets the foundation for understanding how to harness these tools for fine-tuning large language models. In the chapters that follow, we will explore detailed strategies and practical implementations that build on the capabilities of both PyTorch and Hugging Face to optimize AI performance.

1.4 Book Structure and Learning Objectives

This book is designed to serve as a comprehensive guide for anyone interested in mastering the art and science of fine-tuning large language models (LLMs) using PyTorch and Hugging Face. Whether you are a beginner looking to gain a foundational understanding or an experienced practitioner seeking advanced techniques, this book offers a structured learning path that combines theory with hands-on practice.

Structure of the Book

The book is organized into carefully curated chapters that gradually build your knowledge and skills. Here's an overview of the structure:

- **Chapters 1-3: Introduction and Fundamentals**
  These chapters lay the groundwork by introducing you to the evolution of LLMs, the significance of fine-tuning in AI, and an overview of the PyTorch and Hugging Face ecosystems. They cover basic concepts and set the stage for more advanced topics.
- **Chapters 4-7: Data, Model Building, and Core Techniques**
  In these chapters, you will learn how to prepare and process data, build custom neural network architectures using PyTorch, and implement essential fine-tuning strategies. Topics include data preprocessing, tokenization, and understanding the underlying mechanics of model training.
- **Chapters 8-11: Advanced Fine-Tuning and Optimization**
  These sections dive into advanced techniques such as parameter-efficient methods (e.g., LoRA), hyperparameter optimization, and evaluation metrics. You'll explore methods to further refine your models and ensure they perform optimally for specific applications.
- **Chapters 12-15: Deployment, Ethics, and Real-World Applications**
  Beyond training and fine-tuning, these chapters address the challenges of scaling, deploying, and integrating models into production environments. They also discuss ethical considerations, bias mitigation, and present real-world case studies that illustrate the practical impact of these techniques.

- **Chapter 16: Future Directions and Conclusion**
  The final chapter provides insights into emerging trends and future research directions in the field of fine-tuning LLMs. It also summarizes key takeaways and offers guidance on continuous learning and community engagement.

Below is a visual representation in the form of a table to help you understand the book's structure:

Section	Focus Area	Key Topics Covered
Introduction and Fundamentals	Evolution of LLMs, Fine-Tuning Importance, Ecosystems Overview	History, basic concepts, introduction to PyTorch & Hugging Face
Data Preparation & Core Techniques	Data cleaning, model building, core fine-tuning methods	Data preprocessing, tokenization, supervised fine-tuning
Advanced Techniques & Optimization	Advanced fine-tuning, hyperparameter optimization, evaluation metrics	Parameter-efficient methods, optimization strategies
Deployment & Real-World Applications	Scaling, deployment, ethical considerations, case studies	Production integration, bias mitigation, case studies

Future Directions & Conclusion	Emerging trends, continuous learning, community engagement	Future research, summary, ongoing learning tips

Table 1.4: Overview of Book Structure

Learning Objectives

By the end of this book, you should be able to:

1. **Understand the Evolution of LLMs and Their Impact on AI:**
   Gain insight into the historical development of language models—from rule-based systems to modern transformer architectures—and appreciate the importance of fine-tuning in achieving specialized performance.
2. **Set Up and Navigate the PyTorch and Hugging Face Ecosystems:**
   Develop proficiency in using PyTorch for building custom neural networks and Hugging Face for accessing and utilizing pre-trained models, datasets, and tokenizers.
3. **Prepare and Process Data for Fine-Tuning:**
   Learn the essential steps in data curation, cleaning, and tokenization, and understand how to effectively prepare domain-specific datasets for model training.
4. **Implement Core and Advanced Fine-Tuning Techniques:**
   Acquire practical skills to fine-tune models on specific tasks. You will explore both supervised learning techniques and advanced methods such as parameter-efficient fine-tuning, enabling you to customize models for diverse applications.
5. **Optimize and Evaluate Model Performance:**
   Understand the principles of hyperparameter optimization, evaluation metrics, and performance monitoring. You will be able to assess model accuracy, robustness, and fairness in real-world scenarios.
6. **Deploy and Integrate Fine-Tuned Models into Production:**
   Gain knowledge on scaling models, deploying them as APIs or microservices, and integrating them into existing systems while ensuring high performance and low latency.
7. **Address Ethical, Fairness, and Bias Considerations:**
   Recognize the importance of ethical AI practices and learn strategies to mitigate bias, ensuring that your models are not only effective but also responsible and fair.

8. **Explore Future Trends and Engage with the AI Community:**
   Stay informed about emerging research, techniques, and best practices in AI. The book encourages ongoing learning and community participation to keep your skills relevant in a rapidly evolving field.

Code Examples and Hands-On Exercises

Throughout the book, you will encounter practical code examples and hands-on exercises that illustrate key concepts. These examples are designed to be complete, accurate, and easy to follow, ensuring that you can replicate and experiment with them on your own. Each code snippet is accompanied by clear explanations that detail every step of the process, from setup and data handling to model training and evaluation.

The structure of this book is tailored to provide a logical progression from fundamental concepts to advanced techniques, ensuring a deep and practical understanding of fine-tuning LLMs. With clearly defined learning objectives, you will be equipped not only with theoretical knowledge but also with the practical skills necessary to optimize AI performance using PyTorch and Hugging Face. As you move through each chapter, you will build a robust toolkit that prepares you to tackle real-world challenges and contribute to the evolving landscape of AI.

Chapter 2: Foundations of Deep Learning and LLMs

2.1 Neural Networks and Deep Learning Basics

Neural networks and deep learning form the backbone of modern artificial intelligence. In this section, we will introduce the fundamental concepts behind neural networks, explain how they work, and illustrate the principles of deep learning in a clear and accessible manner.

What is a Neural Network?

A neural network is a computational model inspired by the structure and function of the human brain. It consists of interconnected units called **neurons**, organized in layers. The simplest neural network, often called a **feedforward neural network**, typically includes the following layers:

- **Input Layer:** Receives raw data.
- **Hidden Layer(s):** Performs computations and feature extraction.
- **Output Layer:** Produces the final prediction or classification.

Each neuron receives one or more inputs, processes them using a weighted sum and a bias term, and then applies an **activation function** to produce an output. The activation function introduces non-linearity, enabling the network to learn complex patterns.

Key Components of a Neural Network

1. **Weights and Biases:**
   - **Weights:** Determine the strength of the connection between neurons.
   - **Biases:** Allow the activation function to be shifted left or right, helping the model to fit the data better.
2. **Activation Functions:**
   Activation functions decide whether a neuron should be activated or not by transforming the weighted input. Some common activation functions include:

Activation Function	Formula	Characteristics
Sigmoid	$\sigma(x)=\frac{1}{1+e^{-x}}$	Outputs values between 0 and 1; can cause vanishing gradients.
Tanh	$\tanh(x)=\frac{e^x-e^{-x}}{e^x+e^{-x}}$	Outputs values between -1 and 1; zero-centered but may still suffer from vanishing gradients.
ReLU (Rectified Linear Unit)	$\text{ReLU}(x)=\max(0,x)$	Introduces non-linearity; computationally efficient and helps mitigate vanishing gradients.
Leaky ReLU	$\text{Leaky ReLU}(x)=\max(0.01x,x)$	Variation of ReLU that allows a small gradient when $x<0$.

3.
   Loss Function:
   The loss function measures how far the model's predictions are from the actual values. Common loss functions include Mean Squared Error (MSE) for regression tasks and Cross-Entropy Loss for classification tasks.
4. **Optimization Algorithm:**
   During training, optimization algorithms such as **Stochastic Gradient**

Descent (SGD) or **Adam** adjust the weights and biases to minimize the loss function. This process involves calculating gradients using **backpropagation**.

The Learning Process

1. **Forward Propagation:**
   The input data passes through the network, layer by layer, until it reaches the output layer. At each neuron, the weighted sum of inputs plus bias is computed and then transformed using an activation function.
2. **Loss Calculation:**
   The output is compared to the ground truth using a loss function. The loss quantifies the error in the network's prediction.
3. **Backward Propagation (Backpropagation):**
   The gradients of the loss function with respect to each weight are computed using the chain rule. These gradients indicate the direction in which the weights should be adjusted to reduce the error.
4. **Weight Update:**
   Using an optimizer, the weights and biases are updated. This step is repeated for many iterations (epochs) until the model converges to a solution that minimizes the loss.

Code Example: Building a Simple Neural Network with PyTorch

Below is an example of a simple feedforward neural network using PyTorch. This example demonstrates a network that learns to classify data into two categories.

python

```python
import torch

import torch.nn as nn

import torch.optim as optim

from sklearn.datasets import make_classification

from sklearn.model_selection import train_test_split
```

```python
from sklearn.preprocessing import StandardScaler


# Generate a synthetic binary classification dataset

X, y = make_classification(n_samples=1000, n_features=20, n_classes=2,
random_state=42)


# Split dataset into training and test sets

X_train, X_test, y_train, y_test = train_test_split(X, y, test_size=0.2,
random_state=42)


# Standardize the features

scaler = StandardScaler()

X_train = scaler.fit_transform(X_train)

X_test = scaler.transform(X_test)


# Convert the data to PyTorch tensors

X_train_tensor = torch.tensor(X_train, dtype=torch.float32)

y_train_tensor = torch.tensor(y_train, dtype=torch.long)

X_test_tensor = torch.tensor(X_test, dtype=torch.float32)

y_test_tensor = torch.tensor(y_test, dtype=torch.long)


# Define a simple neural network class

class SimpleNN(nn.Module):

    def __init__(self, input_size, hidden_size, output_size):
```

```python
        super(SimpleNN, self).__init__()
        self.fc1 = nn.Linear(input_size, hidden_size)
        self.relu = nn.ReLU()
        self.fc2 = nn.Linear(hidden_size, output_size)


    def forward(self, x):
        x = self.fc1(x)
        x = self.relu(x)
        x = self.fc2(x)
        return x


# Create a model instance
model = SimpleNN(input_size=20, hidden_size=10, output_size=2)


# Define a loss function and an optimizer
criterion = nn.CrossEntropyLoss()
optimizer = optim.Adam(model.parameters(), lr=0.001)


# Training loop
num_epochs = 20
for epoch in range(num_epochs):
    # Forward pass: compute predicted outputs by passing inputs to the
model
    outputs = model(X_train_tensor)
```

```python
    # Calculate the loss
    loss = criterion(outputs, y_train_tensor)

    # Backward pass: compute gradient of the loss with respect to model parameters
    optimizer.zero_grad()
    loss.backward()

    # Update parameters
    optimizer.step()

    if (epoch+1) % 5 == 0:
        print(f"Epoch [{epoch+1}/{num_epochs}], Loss: {loss.item():.4f}")

# Evaluate the model on the test set
with torch.no_grad():
    test_outputs = model(X_test_tensor)
    _, predicted = torch.max(test_outputs, 1)
    accuracy = (predicted == y_test_tensor).float().mean()
    print(f"Test Accuracy: {accuracy:.4f}")
```

Explanation:

- **Data Preparation:**
  We generate a synthetic dataset for binary classification and split it into training and test sets. Standardization is applied to normalize the features, which helps in training the neural network.
- **Tensor Conversion:**
  The NumPy arrays are converted into PyTorch tensors, which are the primary data structure used in PyTorch for model training.
- **Model Definition:**
  The SimpleNN class defines a feedforward neural network with one hidden layer. The ReLU activation function introduces non-linearity between the input and output layers.
- **Loss and Optimization:**
  We use the Cross-Entropy Loss function for classification and the Adam optimizer to update the model's parameters.
- **Training Loop:**
  The training loop runs for a specified number of epochs. In each epoch, a forward pass computes the model's predictions, the loss is calculated, and gradients are computed via backpropagation. The optimizer then updates the weights.
- **Evaluation:**
  After training, the model's performance is evaluated on the test set by comparing the predicted class labels with the true labels.

Understanding the basics of neural networks and deep learning is essential for mastering advanced techniques in fine-tuning large language models. This section introduced the key components of neural networks—including weights, biases, activation functions, loss functions, and optimization methods—and provided a clear explanation of the learning process involving forward and backward propagation. The included code example demonstrates how these concepts are applied in a practical setting using PyTorch.

With this solid foundation, you are now prepared to explore more complex architectures and techniques that underpin modern deep learning and natural language processing. In the following sections, we will build upon these basics to delve deeper into the world of large language models and their fine-tuning.

2.2 Understanding Pre-Training vs. Fine-Tuning

In the field of deep learning, especially when working with large language models (LLMs), two critical phases define the training process: **pre-training** and **fine-tuning**. Both are essential but serve different purposes and are carried out at different stages of model development. In this section, we will explain these phases in detail, highlighting their roles, benefits, and differences.

Pre-Training: Building a Generalist Model

Pre-training is the initial phase where a model learns from a vast and diverse dataset. The main objective during pre-training is to help the model capture a wide range of language patterns, structures, and general knowledge. Here are the key aspects:

- **Purpose:**
  The primary goal is to develop a strong general-purpose model that understands language broadly. The model learns linguistic structures, common sense reasoning, and contextual relationships without being biased toward a specific task or domain.
- **Data:**
  Pre-training uses massive, unannotated datasets collected from sources such as books, articles, and websites. The diversity of this data allows the model to learn from a wide spectrum of topics and styles.
- **Learning Approach:**
  Typically, unsupervised or self-supervised learning methods are employed. For example, models like BERT are pre-trained using a masked language modeling task (predicting masked words), while GPT models use a next-word prediction objective.
- **Output:**
  The outcome of pre-training is a model with robust language representations. This model has learned general language features but is not yet specialized for any particular task.

Fine-Tuning: Specializing the Model

Fine-tuning is the subsequent phase where the pre-trained model is adapted to a specific task or domain using a smaller, task-specific dataset. The goal here is to refine the general model so that it excels in a particular application.

- **Purpose:**
  Fine-tuning tailors the model's capabilities to a defined task, such as sentiment analysis, question answering, or machine translation. It allows the model to incorporate task-specific knowledge and nuances.
- **Data:**
  Fine-tuning is performed on a relatively smaller and highly curated dataset that is relevant to the target task. This dataset is typically labeled, ensuring that the model learns from high-quality, domain-specific examples.

- **Learning Approach:**
  During fine-tuning, supervised learning methods are usually employed. The pre-trained model's weights are adjusted based on the new data, often with a lower learning rate to prevent the loss of general language understanding.
- **Output:**
  The result of fine-tuning is a specialized model that performs exceptionally well on the intended task while still benefiting from the comprehensive language understanding acquired during pre-training.

Comparative Overview

Below is a table that summarizes the key differences between pre-training and fine-tuning:

Aspect	Pre-Training	Fine-Tuning
Objective	Learn general language representations	Adapt the model for a specific task or domain
Data Used	Large, diverse, and mostly unlabeled datasets	Smaller, curated, and task-specific (often labeled) datasets
Learning Method	Unsupervised or self-supervised (e.g., masked language modeling, next-word prediction)	Supervised learning using labeled data

Focus	Broad understanding of language and context	Task-specific knowledge and nuances
Model Outcome	A general-purpose language model	A specialized model with fine-tuned parameters for a specific application
Training Duration	Typically long due to the large size of data	Shorter, as it involves updating an already pre-trained model

Table 2.1: Comparison of Pre-Training and Fine-Tuning

Code Example: Transitioning from Pre-Training to Fine-Tuning

Let's walk through a simplified example using the Hugging Face Transformers library. In this example, we first load a pre-trained model and then fine-tune it on a custom dataset for a text classification task.

python

```python
from transformers import AutoTokenizer,
AutoModelForSequenceClassification, Trainer, TrainingArguments

from datasets import load_dataset

# Load a pre-trained model and tokenizer (e.g., BERT)

model_name = "bert-base-uncased"
```

```python
tokenizer = AutoTokenizer.from_pretrained(model_name)

model =
AutoModelForSequenceClassification.from_pretrained(model_name,
num_labels=2)


# Load a sample dataset for text classification

# For this example, we use the 'imdb' dataset available in the Hugging Face
Datasets library

dataset = load_dataset("imdb")

# Use a small subset for demonstration purposes

train_dataset = dataset["train"].shuffle(seed=42).select(range(1000))

test_dataset = dataset["test"].shuffle(seed=42).select(range(1000))


# Tokenization function for fine-tuning

def tokenize_function(examples):

    return tokenizer(examples["text"], padding="max_length",
truncation=True)


# Tokenize the datasets
```

2.3 Transformer Architecture Fundamentals

The Transformer architecture, introduced in the seminal paper "Attention Is All You Need," represents a revolutionary approach to processing sequential data such as text. Unlike traditional recurrent neural networks (RNNs) or convolutional neural networks (CNNs) that process data sequentially or locally, Transformers leverage self-attention mechanisms to handle long-range dependencies in a highly parallelizable manner. In this section, we will explore the core components of the Transformer architecture, explaining each in clear and simple terms while providing illustrative code examples and tables.

Key Components of the Transformer

The Transformer is primarily composed of the following building blocks:

1. **Input Embeddings and Positional Encoding**
2. **Self-Attention Mechanism**
3. **Multi-Head Attention**
4. **Feed-Forward Neural Networks (FFN)**
5. **Residual Connections and Layer Normalization**
6. **Encoder-Decoder Structure (for sequence-to-sequence tasks)**

Each of these components plays a crucial role in enabling the Transformer to learn and represent complex relationships within the input data.

1. Input Embeddings and Positional Encoding

Input Embeddings:
Before processing text, words are converted into vectors—a process known as embedding. These embeddings capture semantic information about the words.

Positional Encoding:
Since the Transformer processes input data in parallel (i.e., without sequential recurrence), it lacks inherent information about the order of the tokens. Positional encodings are added to the input embeddings to inject information about the relative or absolute position of tokens in the sequence.

A common positional encoding formula is based on sine and cosine functions:

PE(pos,2i)=sin⁡(pos100002i/dmodel)PE(pos,2i)=sin(100002i/dmodelpos)PE(pos,2i+1)=cos⁡(pos100002i/dmodel)PE(pos,2i+1)=cos(100002i/dmodelpos)

where:

- pospos is the token position,
- ii is the dimension index,
- dmodeldmodel is the model's embedding dimension.

2. Self-Attention Mechanism

Self-attention allows the model to weigh the importance of different words in a sentence relative to one another. For each word (token) in the input, self-attention computes a weighted sum of the representations of all tokens in the sequence.

Steps in Self-Attention:

1. **Query, Key, and Value Vectors:**
   The input embeddings are linearly transformed into three vectors: queries QQ, keys KK, and values VV.
2. **Attention Scores:**
   The attention score for a pair of tokens is computed as the dot product between the query of one token and the key of another, scaled by $dkdk$ (where $dkdk$ is the dimension of the key vectors):
   $$Attention(Q,K,V) = softmax\left(\frac{QKT}{dk}\right)V \quad Attention(Q,K,V) = softmax(dkQKT)V$$
3. **Weighted Sum:**
   The softmax function converts the scores to probabilities, which are then used to weight the values VV. This produces the output for each token.

3. Multi-Head Attention

Instead of performing a single attention function, the Transformer uses multiple "heads" of attention. Each head performs self-attention independently, capturing different aspects of the relationships between words. The outputs of all heads are then concatenated and projected to form the final output.

Benefits of Multi-Head Attention:

- **Diverse Representation:** Each head can focus on different types of relationships.
- **Improved Learning:** Allows the model to learn complex patterns by attending to different parts of the input simultaneously.

4. Feed-Forward Neural Networks (FFN)

After the attention mechanism, the Transformer applies a position-wise feed-forward network. This network is applied independently to each position (token) and typically consists of two linear transformations with a ReLU activation in between:

$$FFN(x)=\max(0,xW_1+b_1)W_2+b_2FFN(x)=\max(0,xW_1+b_1)W_2+b_2$$

This component introduces non-linearity and further processes the attended information.

5. Residual Connections and Layer Normalization

To facilitate training deep networks, Transformers use residual (skip) connections around each sub-layer (attention and FFN). This means that the input to a sub-layer is added to its output, helping gradients flow through the network more effectively.

After adding the residual connection, **layer normalization** is applied to stabilize and accelerate training by normalizing the outputs across the features.

6. Encoder-Decoder Structure

While some Transformer models, like BERT, use only the encoder part for understanding tasks, others, like the original Transformer or T5, employ an encoder-decoder structure for tasks such as translation. In this architecture:

- **Encoder:** Processes the input sequence and produces a set of representations.
- **Decoder:** Uses these representations, along with self-attention, to generate the output sequence.

Comparative Table of Transformer Components

Component	Function	Key Characteristics
Input Embeddings	Converts tokens into dense vector representations	Captures semantic meaning; initial layer

		for all subsequent processing
Positional Encoding	Adds sequence order information to embeddings	Uses sine/cosine functions; enables parallel processing
Self-Attention	Weighs the importance of each token relative to others	Computes attention scores; handles long-range dependencies
Multi-Head Attention	Implements multiple self-attention mechanisms in parallel	Diversifies the focus; improves pattern recognition
Feed-Forward Networks	Applies non-linear transformations to each token independently	Consists of two linear layers with an activation function
Residual & Norm Layers	Facilitates gradient flow and stabilizes training	Adds input to output; normalizes feature distributions
Encoder-Decoder Structure	Separates the processing of input and output sequences for tasks like translation	Encoder for understanding, decoder for generation

Table 2.2: Overview of Transformer Architecture Components

Code Example: Simplified Transformer Encoder Block in PyTorch

The following code example provides a simplified implementation of a Transformer encoder block using PyTorch. This block includes multi-head attention, a feed-forward network, residual connections, and layer normalization.

python

```python
import torch

import torch.nn as nn

import math


class MultiHeadSelfAttention(nn.Module):
    def __init__(self, d_model, num_heads):
        super(MultiHeadSelfAttention, self).__init__()
        assert d_model % num_heads == 0, "d_model must be divisible by num_heads"


        self.d_model = d_model
        self.num_heads = num_heads
        self.d_k = d_model // num_heads


        self.q_linear = nn.Linear(d_model, d_model)

        self.k_linear = nn.Linear(d_model, d_model)

        self.v_linear = nn.Linear(d_model, d_model)
```

41

```python
        self.out_linear = nn.Linear(d_model, d_model)


    def forward(self, x):
        batch_size, seq_length, d_model = x.size()


        # Linear projections
        Q = self.q_linear(x)  # (batch_size, seq_length, d_model)
        K = self.k_linear(x)
        V = self.v_linear(x)


        # Split into multiple heads
        Q = Q.view(batch_size, seq_length, self.num_heads,
self.d_k).transpose(1, 2)
        K = K.view(batch_size, seq_length, self.num_heads,
self.d_k).transpose(1, 2)
        V = V.view(batch_size, seq_length, self.num_heads,
self.d_k).transpose(1, 2)


        # Scaled Dot-Product Attention
        scores = torch.matmul(Q, K.transpose(-2, -1)) / math.sqrt(self.d_k)
        attn_weights = torch.softmax(scores, dim=-1)
        attn_output = torch.matmul(attn_weights, V)


        # Concatenate heads and put through final linear layer
```

```python
        attn_output = attn_output.transpose(1,
2).contiguous().view(batch_size, seq_length, d_model)

        output = self.out_linear(attn_output)

        return output


class TransformerEncoderBlock(nn.Module):
    def __init__(self, d_model, num_heads, d_ff, dropout=0.1):
        super(TransformerEncoderBlock, self).__init__()
        self.attention = MultiHeadSelfAttention(d_model, num_heads)
        self.layer_norm1 = nn.LayerNorm(d_model)
        self.feed_forward = nn.Sequential(
            nn.Linear(d_model, d_ff),
            nn.ReLU(),
            nn.Linear(d_ff, d_model)
        )
        self.layer_norm2 = nn.LayerNorm(d_model)
        self.dropout = nn.Dropout(dropout)


    def forward(self, x):
        # Multi-head self-attention with residual connection and layer
normalization
        attn_output = self.attention(x)
        x = self.layer_norm1(x + self.dropout(attn_output))
```

```python
    # Feed-forward network with residual connection and layer
normalization

    ff_output = self.feed_forward(x)

    x = self.layer_norm2(x + self.dropout(ff_output))

    return x


# Example usage:
batch_size = 2
seq_length = 5
d_model = 32
num_heads = 4
d_ff = 64


# Random input tensor representing embedded tokens
x = torch.rand(batch_size, seq_length, d_model)


# Create a Transformer encoder block
encoder_block = TransformerEncoderBlock(d_model, num_heads, d_ff)
output = encoder_block(x)


print("Input shape:", x.shape)
print("Output shape:", output.shape)
```

Explanation:

- **MultiHeadSelfAttention Class:**
  This class defines the multi-head self-attention mechanism.
  - It projects the input xx into query, key, and value vectors.
  - The vectors are split into multiple heads to allow the model to focus on different aspects of the input.
  - Scaled dot-product attention is computed for each head, and the results are concatenated and projected back to the original dimension.
- **TransformerEncoderBlock Class:**
  This block combines multi-head self-attention with a feed-forward network.
  - **Residual Connections:** After the attention and feed-forward sub-layers, the input is added back (with dropout applied) and normalized.
  - **Layer Normalization:** Helps stabilize the training by normalizing the outputs of each sub-layer.
- **Example Usage:**
  We create a random input tensor simulating a batch of token embeddings and pass it through the encoder block. The printed shapes confirm that the output retains the same dimensions as the input.

The Transformer architecture has revolutionized the way we approach sequence processing by replacing recurrent mechanisms with self-attention and multi-head attention. This design allows for efficient, parallelized training and the ability to capture long-range dependencies in data. Understanding these fundamentals—input embeddings with positional encodings, self-attention, multi-head mechanisms, feed-forward networks, and the role of residual connections and normalization—is crucial for appreciating modern natural language processing systems.

The code example provided offers a hands-on look at how these concepts are implemented in PyTorch, bridging theory with practice. With this foundation, you are now prepared to explore more advanced topics in fine-tuning and deploying large language models in the chapters that follow.

2.4 Case Studies: Milestones in LLM Development

The evolution of large language models (LLMs) is marked by a series of groundbreaking milestones. Each milestone represents significant advancements in model architecture, training techniques, or application performance that have shaped modern natural language processing. In this section, we present detailed case studies of these pivotal developments, providing context, key innovations, and their lasting impact on the field.

Early Foundations: Rule-Based and Statistical Models

Overview:
Before the advent of neural networks, language processing relied on rule-based systems and statistical models such as n-gram models. These early methods, while limited by their inability to capture deep contextual relationships, laid the groundwork for understanding language patterns.

Key Contributions:

- **Rule-Based Systems:** Used handcrafted rules to parse language.
- **Statistical Models (n-grams):** Predicted words based on fixed-length context windows, introducing probabilistic language modeling.

Impact:
These early approaches highlighted the challenges of capturing context and paved the way for the development of more sophisticated, data-driven models.

The Transformer Breakthrough (2017)

Case Study: "Attention Is All You Need"
In 2017, the publication of the paper "Attention Is All You Need" by Vaswani et al. revolutionized NLP. The Transformer architecture introduced self-attention mechanisms, which allowed models to process all tokens in a sequence simultaneously, effectively capturing long-range dependencies without the sequential limitations of recurrent models.

Key Contributions:

- **Self-Attention:** Enabled the model to weigh the importance of different words in a sentence.
- **Parallel Processing:** Allowed for more efficient training on modern hardware.
- **Scalability:** Set the stage for building larger models with improved performance.

Impact:
Transformers have become the backbone of most state-of-the-art LLMs. They have enabled significant improvements in tasks like machine translation, text summarization, and question answering.

BERT: Bidirectional Encoder Representations from Transformers (2018)

Case Study: BERT (Google)

BERT was introduced in 2018 as a model that could understand context in both directions (left-to-right and right-to-left). This bidirectional training allowed BERT to achieve state-of-the-art performance on a variety of NLP benchmarks.

Key Contributions:

- **Bidirectional Context:** Unlike previous models that processed text in a single direction, BERT's bidirectional approach provided a deeper understanding of language context.
- **Masked Language Modeling:** The training task of predicting masked tokens helped BERT learn robust contextual representations.
- **Versatility:** BERT was fine-tuned for various downstream tasks such as sentiment analysis, named entity recognition, and question answering.

Impact:

BERT's success inspired a wave of transformer-based models and fine-tuning strategies, significantly influencing subsequent developments in LLMs.

GPT Series: Generative Pre-Trained Transformers (2018-Present)

Case Study: GPT-2 and GPT-3 (OpenAI)

OpenAI's GPT series represents another milestone in LLM development. Starting with GPT-2 in 2018 and advancing to GPT-3 in 2020, these models demonstrated the power of scaling up transformer architectures.

Key Contributions:

- **Unsupervised Pre-Training:** GPT models are pre-trained on vast amounts of text data using a next-word prediction objective.
- **Scale:** GPT-3, with 175 billion parameters, showcased the ability to generate coherent, contextually relevant text across diverse topics.
- **Versatility in Applications:** From chatbots to creative writing, the GPT series has been adapted to a wide range of applications through fine-tuning and prompt engineering.

Impact:

The GPT series has dramatically pushed the boundaries of what is possible with LLMs, highlighting the benefits of large-scale pre-training and the potential for generative applications.

Comparative Milestones Table

Below is a table summarizing key milestones in the development of LLMs:

Time Period	Model/Approach	Key Innovations	Impact
1950s – 1980s	Rule-Based and Statistical Models	Handcrafted rules; n-gram statistical methods	Laid the foundation for language modeling
2017	Transformer (Vaswani et al.)	Self-attention; parallel processing; scalability	Revolutionized model architecture; enabled large-scale models
2018	BERT (Google)	Bidirectional training; masked language modeling	Set new benchmarks; versatile for various NLP tasks
2018 – Present	GPT Series (OpenAI: GPT-2, GPT-3)	Unsupervised pre-training; massive scale; generative capabilities	Expanded the range of LLM applications; demonstrated power of scaling

Table 2.2: Milestones in LLM Development

Code Example: Using a Pre-Trained Model (BERT) for Sentiment Analysis

To illustrate the impact of these milestones, consider this simple example using a pre-trained BERT model from the Hugging Face Transformers library to perform sentiment analysis:

python

```python
from transformers import pipeline

# Load the sentiment-analysis pipeline with a pre-trained BERT model
sentiment_pipeline = pipeline("sentiment-analysis",
model="nlptown/bert-base-multilingual-uncased-sentiment")

# Sample texts for sentiment analysis
texts = [
    "I absolutely loved the movie! It was fantastic and moving.",
    "The product was mediocre and did not meet my expectations."
]

# Perform sentiment analysis
results = sentiment_pipeline(texts)

# Print the results
for text, result in zip(texts, results):
    print(f"Input Text: {text}")
```

```python
    print(f"Sentiment: {result['label']} (Confidence: {result['score']:.2f})")

    print("-" * 50)
```

Explanation:

- **Pipeline Loading:**
  The pipeline function from Hugging Face simplifies the process of loading a pre-trained model. Here, a multilingual BERT model fine-tuned for sentiment analysis is used.
- **Input Texts:**
  Two sample texts are analyzed, one with positive sentiment and the other with negative sentiment.
- **Results:**
  The pipeline outputs sentiment labels (e.g., positive, negative) along with confidence scores, demonstrating how pre-trained models can be directly applied to real-world tasks.

The journey of LLM development is rich with transformative milestones—from early rule-based systems to the powerful Transformer architectures that dominate modern NLP. Each milestone has contributed unique innovations that have collectively advanced our ability to understand and generate human language. By studying these case studies, we gain insights into the evolution of AI models, appreciate the underlying innovations, and understand the impact these developments have had on a wide range of applications. As you progress through this book, you will see how these foundational breakthroughs inform the techniques and strategies for fine-tuning LLMs to achieve superior performance in specific tasks.

Chapter 3: Setting Up Your Environment

A successful journey into fine-tuning large language models begins with setting up a robust and efficient development environment. This chapter covers the essential hardware and software requirements and guides you through the installation of PyTorch and other critical libraries. By ensuring that your system is properly configured, you can focus on building and optimizing models without facing compatibility or performance issues.

3.1 Hardware and Software Requirements

Before diving into model training and fine-tuning, it is important to understand the hardware and software prerequisites. This section outlines the key components and their roles in building an effective AI development environment.

Hardware Requirements

When working with large language models, hardware plays a crucial role in determining both training speed and efficiency. Here are the primary hardware components to consider:

- **Central Processing Unit (CPU):**
  A powerful CPU is necessary for managing overall system operations and handling tasks that do not require parallel processing. While a high-end CPU is beneficial, most deep learning tasks are offloaded to the GPU.
- **Graphics Processing Unit (GPU):**
  GPUs are essential for accelerating the training of deep neural networks. They provide parallel processing capabilities that significantly reduce training time. NVIDIA GPUs are most commonly used due to their robust support for deep learning libraries such as PyTorch.
- **Memory (RAM):**
  Sufficient RAM is needed to load large datasets and manage computations. A minimum of 16 GB is recommended for most deep learning tasks, though larger models or datasets may require 32 GB or more.
- **Storage:**
  Fast storage solutions like SSDs (Solid State Drives) are preferred for quicker data access and reduced load times. The capacity should be determined by the size of your datasets and models; typically, 512 GB to 1 TB is a good starting point.

Below is a table summarizing the recommended hardware specifications:

Component	Minimum Requirement	Recommended	Role in Deep Learning
CPU	Quad-core Intel/AMD	6-8 cores or more	Overall system operations, preprocessing tasks
GPU	NVIDIA GPU with 4 GB VRAM	NVIDIA RTX series (6 GB+ VRAM)	Accelerates training via parallel processing
RAM	16 GB	32 GB or more	Loads datasets and manages computations efficiently
Storage	256 GB SSD (or HDD)	512 GB to 1 TB SSD	Fast data access and storage of large models and datasets

Software Requirements

A properly configured software environment is equally important. Here are the key software components and their roles:

- **Operating System (OS):**
  Linux (e.g., Ubuntu) and Windows are both supported for deep learning development. Linux is often preferred for its performance and compatibility with various deep learning tools.

- **Python:**
  Python is the predominant language in AI and deep learning. It is recommended to use Python 3.7 or later.
- **Package Management:**
  Tools like **pip** and **conda** help manage Python packages and environments. They ensure that all dependencies are compatible and can be isolated to prevent conflicts.
- **Deep Learning Libraries:**
  - **PyTorch:** A widely used deep learning framework.
  - **Hugging Face Transformers:** Provides access to pre-trained models and fine-tuning utilities.
  - **Additional Libraries:** NumPy, Pandas, Scikit-Learn, and Matplotlib are commonly used for data manipulation and visualization.

Below is a table summarizing the recommended software components:

Software Component	Version/Specification	Purpose
Operating System	Ubuntu 18.04/20.04 or Windows 10	Core platform for development
Python	3.7 or later	Primary programming language for deep learning
Package Manager	pip or conda	Dependency management and environment isolation

Deep Learning Framework	PyTorch (latest stable release)	Building and training neural network models
NLP Libraries	Hugging Face Transformers (latest)	Access to pre-trained models and fine-tuning pipelines
Data Manipulation Libraries	NumPy, Pandas, Scikit-Learn, Matplotlib	Data preprocessing, analysis, and visualization

3.2 Installing PyTorch and Essential Libraries

Once you have reviewed the hardware and software requirements, the next step is to install the necessary tools. This section provides step-by-step instructions for installing PyTorch and other essential libraries. The instructions include code examples and command-line snippets to ensure accuracy and clarity.

Installing PyTorch

PyTorch can be installed using either pip or conda. Visit the official PyTorch website to customize the installation command based on your operating system, package manager, and whether you are using a GPU. Below are example commands for both methods:

Using pip

For a typical installation on Linux or Windows with GPU support (assuming an NVIDIA GPU with CUDA), you might use:

bash

```
pip install torch torchvision torchaudio --extra-index-url
https://download.pytorch.org/whl/cu117
```

Explanation:

- torch: The core PyTorch library.
- torchvision: Provides datasets, model architectures, and image transformations for computer vision tasks.
- torchaudio: Useful for processing audio data.
- --extra-index-url: Specifies the URL for CUDA-enabled PyTorch wheels.

Using conda

If you prefer using conda, the command is similar:

bash

```
conda install pytorch torchvision torchaudio cudatoolkit=11.7 -c pytorch
```

Explanation:

- cudatoolkit=11.7: Specifies the version of CUDA to match your GPU drivers.
- -c pytorch: Indicates that the packages should be installed from the official PyTorch channel.

Installing Essential Libraries

In addition to PyTorch, several libraries are essential for data processing, model evaluation, and fine-tuning. These include Hugging Face Transformers, NumPy, Pandas, Scikit-Learn, and Matplotlib. You can install them using pip as follows:

bash

```
pip install transformers numpy pandas scikit-learn matplotlib datasets
```

Explanation:

- transformers: Provides state-of-the-art pre-trained models and fine-tuning utilities.
- numpy: Fundamental package for numerical computations.
- pandas: Data manipulation and analysis library.
- scikit-learn: Machine learning library for data preprocessing, model evaluation, and utility functions.
- matplotlib: Visualization library for plotting data.
- datasets: Hugging Face library for accessing and processing datasets.

Verifying Your Installation

After installing the necessary packages, it is good practice to verify that everything is set up correctly. You can run a simple script to check the installation:

python

```python
import torch

import transformers

import numpy as np

import pandas as pd

import sklearn

import matplotlib.pyplot as plt


print("PyTorch version:", torch.__version__)

print("Transformers version:", transformers.__version__)

print("NumPy version:", np.__version__)

print("Pandas version:", pd.__version__)

print("Scikit-Learn version:", sklearn.__version__)

print("Matplotlib version:", plt.__version__)
```

Explanation:

- This script imports each of the installed libraries and prints their version numbers.
- If all libraries load correctly and display version information, your environment is properly configured for further development.

Setting up your environment with the right hardware and software is the first critical step in working with large language models and fine-tuning techniques. By ensuring you have a powerful GPU, sufficient memory, and a modern OS, along with installing the latest versions of PyTorch, Hugging Face Transformers, and other essential libraries, you are well-prepared to start your deep learning projects. The detailed instructions and code examples provided in this chapter will help you build a stable and efficient environment, paving the way for advanced model development and experimentation in the chapters to come.

3.3 Navigating the Hugging Face Ecosystem

The Hugging Face ecosystem is a vibrant and expansive community dedicated to advancing natural language processing (NLP) and machine learning. It provides a suite of tools and libraries that simplify model discovery, fine-tuning, and deployment. In this section, we will explore the key components of the Hugging Face ecosystem and provide guidance on how to navigate its resources effectively.

Key Components of the Hugging Face Ecosystem

1. **Transformers Library**
   The Transformers library is the cornerstone of the Hugging Face ecosystem. It offers a unified interface for a wide variety of pre-trained models, including BERT, GPT, T5, RoBERTa, and more. These models can be used directly for tasks such as text classification, translation, question answering, and text generation.
   - **Features:**
     - Easy model loading using the from_pretrained() method
     - Built-in pipelines for common tasks
     - Compatibility with both PyTorch and TensorFlow
2. **Datasets Library**
   This library simplifies the process of accessing, processing, and sharing datasets. It supports a multitude of datasets relevant to NLP and beyond.
   - **Features:**
     - Direct integration with Hugging Face Hub for quick dataset downloads
     - Tools for dataset splitting, shuffling, and filtering

- Support for various data formats and efficient data caching

3. **Tokenizers Library**

Efficient tokenization is critical for preparing text data. The Tokenizers library provides fast, optimized tokenization tools that support multiple languages and encoding strategies.

- o **Features:**
  - Highly optimized in Rust for performance
  - Supports byte-pair encoding (BPE), WordPiece, and more
  - Easily integrates with the Transformers library

4. **Model Hub**

The Hugging Face Model Hub is an online repository where users can share, download, and collaborate on models. It hosts thousands of pre-trained models contributed by both Hugging Face and the community.

- o **Features:**
  - Model versioning and detailed model cards explaining usage, training data, and evaluation metrics
  - Easy integration into code via the Transformers library
  - Search and filter functionalities to quickly find models for your specific use case

5. **Community and Documentation**

Hugging Face maintains comprehensive documentation, tutorials, and an active community forum. Whether you are a beginner or an expert, these resources help you troubleshoot issues and learn best practices.

- o **Resources:**
  - Official documentation and quickstart guides
  - Interactive tutorials and notebooks on platforms like Google Colab
  - Community discussions on forums and GitHub repositories

Navigating the Ecosystem: Practical Tips

- **Start with Pipelines:**
  Hugging Face pipelines offer high-level interfaces for tasks like sentiment analysis or text generation. They let you experiment quickly without needing to manage complex configurations.
- **Explore the Model Hub:**
  Use the Model Hub website to search for models relevant to your domain. Read the accompanying model cards to understand the model's strengths, limitations, and recommended use cases.
- **Leverage Tutorials and Examples:**
  Hugging Face provides a wealth of examples in their documentation and on

GitHub. These examples demonstrate how to fine-tune models, use the datasets library, and even deploy models to production.

- **Join the Community:**
  Engage with the Hugging Face community through their forums and social media channels. This is an excellent way to stay updated on new developments and receive assistance when needed.

Code Example: Using a Pipeline for Text Generation

Below is a simple example that demonstrates how to use the Hugging Face Transformers library to perform text generation using a pre-trained model from the Model Hub:

python

```python
from transformers import pipeline

# Create a text generation pipeline using GPT-2

text_generator = pipeline("text-generation", model="gpt2")

# Define a prompt for text generation

prompt = "The future of artificial intelligence is"

# Generate text with a specified maximum length and number of sequences

generated_texts = text_generator(prompt, max_length=50,
num_return_sequences=1)

# Print the generated text

print("Generated Text:")

print(generated_texts[0]['generated_text'])
```

Explanation:

- **Pipeline Creation:**
  The pipeline function creates a high-level interface for text generation using the pre-trained GPT-2 model.
- **Text Generation:**
  A prompt is provided, and the model generates a continuation of the text. The parameters max_length and num_return_sequences control the output.
- **Output:**
  The generated text is printed, demonstrating the ease of using pre-trained models for quick experimentation.

3.4 Managing Dependencies with Docker and Virtual Environments

Managing dependencies and ensuring a reproducible development environment are critical steps in any machine learning project. Docker and virtual environments help isolate your project's dependencies, making it easier to avoid conflicts and share your work with others.

Virtual Environments

A virtual environment is a self-contained directory that contains a specific Python version and its associated packages. This allows you to maintain project-specific dependencies without interfering with the system-wide Python installation.

Popular Tools:

- **venv (Standard Library):**
  Comes built-in with Python 3.
- **conda:**
  An open-source package management system that also supports virtual environments.
- **virtualenv:**
  A tool for creating isolated Python environments.

Creating a Virtual Environment with venv:

bash

```
# Create a virtual environment named 'env'

python3 -m venv env
```

```
# Activate the virtual environment (Linux/Mac)

source env/bin/activate
```

```
# Activate the virtual environment (Windows)

env\Scripts\activate
```

```
# Install required libraries

pip install torch transformers datasets numpy pandas scikit-learn
matplotlib
```

Explanation:

- **Creating the Environment:**
  The command creates a folder named env that contains the Python interpreter
  and dependencies.
- **Activating the Environment:**
  The activation command ensures that any packages installed or executed are
  confined to the virtual environment.
- **Installing Dependencies:**
  Installing libraries within the virtual environment ensures a clean, isolated
  workspace.

Docker

Docker is a containerization platform that packages an application and its dependencies
into a single container, ensuring consistency across different development and
production environments.

Benefits of Docker:

- **Reproducibility:**
  Containers behave the same regardless of where they are deployed.
- **Isolation:**
  Each container runs independently, preventing dependency conflicts.
- **Portability:**
  Docker containers can run on any system that supports Docker.

Creating a Dockerfile for a Deep Learning Project:

Below is an example Dockerfile that sets up an environment with Python, PyTorch, and Hugging Face libraries:

Dockerfile

```
# Use an official PyTorch image with CUDA support as the base image

FROM pytorch/pytorch:1.12.0-cuda11.3-cudnn8-runtime


# Set the working directory in the container

WORKDIR /app


# Copy the requirements file into the container

COPY requirements.txt .


# Install the required Python packages

RUN pip install --upgrade pip && \

    pip install -r requirements.txt


# Copy the rest of the application code
```

```
COPY . .
```

```
# Define the command to run your application (e.g., a script called
'main.py')

CMD ["python", "main.py"]
```

requirements.txt Example:

ini

```
transformers==4.21.0

datasets==2.3.2

numpy==1.21.0

pandas==1.3.5

scikit-learn==1.0.2

matplotlib==3.5.1
```

Explanation:

- **Base Image:**
  The Dockerfile starts from an official PyTorch image that includes CUDA support for GPU acceleration.
- **Working Directory:**
  The WORKDIR command sets /app as the directory where all commands will run.
- **Dependency Installation:**
  Dependencies listed in requirements.txt are installed in the container.
- **Copying Files:**
  Application code is copied into the container to ensure all necessary scripts are available.

- **Run Command:**
  The CMD command defines the default command to execute when the container starts.

Running a Docker Container

Once you have written your Dockerfile, you can build and run your container using the following commands:

bash

```
# Build the Docker image and tag it as 'llm-env'

docker build -t llm-env .
```

```
# Run the Docker container

docker run --gpus all -it --rm llm-env
```

Explanation:

- **Building the Image:**
  The docker build command creates an image named llm-env based on the Dockerfile.
- **Running the Container:**
  The docker run command starts a container with GPU access (using --gpus all), attaches an interactive terminal (-it), and removes the container after it stops (--rm).

Navigating the Hugging Face ecosystem and managing dependencies effectively are crucial for a smooth workflow in fine-tuning large language models. The Hugging Face ecosystem offers a robust suite of tools that simplify model discovery, data handling, and fine-tuning, while virtual environments and Docker containers ensure that your development environment remains clean, reproducible, and portable. By mastering these tools, you set a strong foundation for building, testing, and deploying advanced NLP applications.

Chapter 4: Data Preparation and Preprocessing

Successful model training begins with high-quality data. In this chapter, we will explore how to prepare your data effectively for fine-tuning large language models (LLMs). We will focus on two main aspects: curating domain-specific datasets and performing data cleaning, tokenization, and augmentation. A well-prepared dataset ensures that your model not only learns efficiently but also performs accurately in real-world applications.

4.1 Curating Domain-Specific Datasets

Curating domain-specific datasets involves gathering and organizing data that is highly relevant to the particular task or industry you want your model to serve. This targeted approach ensures that the model learns the specialized vocabulary, context, and nuances inherent in the domain.

Steps for Curating Domain-Specific Datasets

1. **Define Your Domain and Objectives:**
   Clearly articulate the industry or task your model will address (e.g., legal, medical, finance, customer service). Identify the specific challenges and requirements unique to this domain.
2. **Source Data:**
   Data can be sourced from publicly available datasets, web scraping, industry reports, or proprietary databases. It is important to ensure that you have the necessary permissions and that the data complies with privacy regulations.
   - **Public Datasets:** Government databases, academic research, or open data initiatives.
   - **Web Scraping:** Use tools like BeautifulSoup or Scrapy to extract data from relevant websites.
   - **Internal Data:** Company records, customer reviews, or specialized documents.
3. **Assess Data Quality:**
   Evaluate the data for completeness, consistency, and relevance. Discard irrelevant or low-quality entries that could degrade the model's performance.
4. **Labeling and Annotation:**
   For supervised tasks, ensure that the dataset is properly labeled. This might involve manual annotation, crowd-sourcing, or semi-automated methods.
   - **Example:** In a legal domain, documents might be labeled as "contract," "brief," or "opinion."

5. **Data Diversity:**
   Ensure that the dataset covers the range of scenarios and variations found within the domain. This includes different writing styles, terminologies, and document types.

Example: Curating a Legal Documents Dataset

Suppose you want to fine-tune an LLM for legal document classification. You might follow these steps:

- **Objective:** Classify documents into categories such as contracts, briefs, and opinions.
- **Data Sources:**
  - Public legal databases (e.g., court opinions)
  - Law firm repositories (with permission)
  - Government archives
- **Quality Checks:**
  - Remove incomplete or scanned documents with poor OCR quality.
  - Verify the accuracy of labels through legal expert review.
- **Annotation:**
  - Use a tool like Prodigy or Labelbox to annotate and verify document categories.

Below is a summary table outlining the curating process:

Step	Key Actions	Tools/Resources
Define Domain & Goals	Identify domain, key challenges, and objectives	Domain research, stakeholder interviews
Source Data	Collect data from public datasets, web scraping, or internal sources	Public datasets, web scraping tools (BeautifulSoup, Scrapy)

Assess Data Quality	Evaluate completeness, relevance, and consistency	Data profiling tools, manual review
Labeling & Annotation	Annotate data with domain-specific labels	Annotation tools (Prodigy, Labelbox)
Ensure Diversity	Cover various document types and styles	Data augmentation, varied data sources

4.2 Data Cleaning, Tokenization, and Augmentation

After curating your dataset, the next crucial steps are data cleaning, tokenization, and augmentation. These processes help prepare the raw text for effective model training by removing noise, converting text into numerical representations, and increasing the dataset's size or diversity.

Data Cleaning

Data cleaning involves preprocessing the raw text to remove inconsistencies and irrelevant information. Key steps include:

- **Removing Noise:**
  Eliminate HTML tags, special characters, extra white spaces, and irrelevant symbols.
- **Handling Missing Values:**
  Identify and address missing or incomplete entries. This may involve removing such entries or filling them with appropriate placeholders.
- **Normalizing Text:**
  Convert text to a uniform format, such as lowercasing, removing punctuation (if appropriate), and standardizing abbreviations.

Code Example: Data Cleaning in Python

Below is an example using Python and the Pandas library to clean a dataset of legal documents:

python

```python
import pandas as pd
import re


# Load dataset (assume a CSV with a 'text' column)
df = pd.read_csv("legal_documents.csv")


# Function to clean text
def clean_text(text):
    # Remove HTML tags
    text = re.sub(r'<.*?>', '', text)
    # Remove non-alphanumeric characters (except spaces)
    text = re.sub(r'[^a-zA-Z0-9\s]', '', text)
    # Convert text to lowercase
    text = text.lower()
    # Remove extra whitespace
    text = re.sub(r'\s+', ' ', text).strip()
    return text


# Apply cleaning function to the text column
```

```python
df['cleaned_text'] = df['text'].apply(clean_text)
```

```python
# Display the first few rows of the cleaned dataset
print(df[['text', 'cleaned_text']].head())
```

Explanation:

- **HTML Tag Removal:**
  The re.sub(r'<.*?>', '', text) function removes any HTML tags.
- **Non-Alphanumeric Removal:**
  The regex r'[^a-zA-Z0-9\s]' removes special characters, preserving alphanumeric characters and spaces.
- **Lowercasing and Whitespace Normalization:**
  Converts all text to lowercase and removes extra spaces.

Tokenization

Tokenization is the process of converting text into tokens, which are the basic units that the model will use. The choice of tokenizer often depends on the model architecture (e.g., BERT, GPT).

- **Subword Tokenization:**
  Methods like Byte-Pair Encoding (BPE) or WordPiece break words into subword units, handling rare words and vocabulary size efficiently.
- **Special Tokens:**
  Tokenizers add special tokens to indicate sentence boundaries, unknown words, or padding for fixed-length sequences.

Code Example: Tokenization with Hugging Face Transformers

Here's how to tokenize a batch of cleaned legal documents using the Hugging Face Transformers library:

python

```python
from transformers import AutoTokenizer
```

```python
# Load a pre-trained tokenizer (e.g., for BERT)

tokenizer = AutoTokenizer.from_pretrained("bert-base-uncased")


# Example text

texts = df['cleaned_text'].tolist()[:5]  # Taking first 5 entries for
demonstration


# Tokenize texts

tokenized_outputs = tokenizer(texts, padding='max_length',
truncation=True, max_length=128, return_tensors="pt")


print("Tokenized Input IDs:")

print(tokenized_outputs['input_ids'])

print("Tokenized Attention Masks:")

print(tokenized_outputs['attention_mask'])
```

Explanation:

- **Tokenizer Loading:**
  Loads a pre-trained tokenizer that matches your model.
- **Tokenization Process:**
  The tokenizer converts text into token IDs, adds padding to a fixed maximum
  length (128 tokens in this case), and creates attention masks to distinguish
  padded tokens from actual content.
- **Return Tensors:**
  Using return_tensors="pt" returns the outputs as PyTorch tensors, ready for
  model input.

Data Augmentation

Data augmentation involves creating additional training examples by modifying existing data. This is especially useful when the dataset is small or when you want to improve model robustness.

- **Text Augmentation Techniques:**
  - ○ **Synonym Replacement:** Replace words with their synonyms.
  - ○ **Random Insertion/Deletion:** Randomly insert or delete words to introduce variability.
  - ○ **Back-Translation:** Translate text to another language and back to the original language.
- **Benefits:**
  Augmentation increases the diversity of the training data, potentially improving model generalization and reducing overfitting.

Code Example: Simple Synonym Replacement

Below is an example using the nlpaug library to perform synonym replacement for data augmentation:

python

```python
import nlpaug.augmenter.word as naw

# Create an augmenter for synonym replacement
aug = naw.SynonymAug(aug_src='wordnet')

# Sample text for augmentation
sample_text = "The contract agreement was legally binding."

# Apply augmentation
augmented_text = aug.augment(sample_text)
```

```
print("Original Text:", sample_text)

print("Augmented Text:", augmented_text)
```

Explanation:

- **Augmenter Initialization:**
  The SynonymAug augmenter replaces words with their synonyms using the
  WordNet lexical database.
- **Augmentation Process:**
  The augment function applies synonym replacement to the sample text.
- **Output:**
  The example displays the original and augmented text, showcasing how
  augmentation can introduce variations.

Data preparation and preprocessing are critical steps in the machine learning pipeline.
Curating domain-specific datasets ensures that your model learns the relevant nuances
of your field, while thorough cleaning, effective tokenization, and strategic data
augmentation enhance the quality and diversity of your training data. By following these
comprehensive steps and leveraging the provided code examples, you can build a robust
dataset that serves as a strong foundation for fine-tuning large language models. With
clean and well-prepared data, you are better positioned to achieve high performance
and reliable results in your domain-specific applications.

4.3 Handling Imbalanced Data and Bias Mitigation

When preparing data for training large language models (LLMs), two challenges often
arise: imbalanced data and inherent biases. Addressing these issues is crucial for
building models that perform fairly and robustly across different scenarios.

Handling Imbalanced Data

Definition and Challenges:
Imbalanced data occurs when some classes (or labels) are significantly
underrepresented compared to others. This imbalance can cause the model to learn a
bias toward the majority class, leading to poor performance on minority classes. For
example, in a sentiment analysis dataset, if 90% of reviews are positive and only 10% are
negative, the model may default to predicting positive sentiment.

Strategies to Address Imbalance:

1. **Resampling Techniques:**
   - **Oversampling:** Increase the number of samples in the minority class. Techniques such as Synthetic Minority Oversampling Technique (SMOTE) create synthetic examples to balance the classes.
   - **Undersampling:** Reduce the number of samples in the majority class. This method can risk losing valuable information if not done carefully.
   - **Combination:** A hybrid approach that combines both oversampling and undersampling to achieve balance.
2. **Algorithm-Level Solutions:**
   - **Class Weighting:** Modify the loss function to penalize misclassification of minority classes more heavily. Many machine learning frameworks, including PyTorch and scikit-learn, allow you to set class weights.
   - **Ensemble Methods:** Use techniques such as bagging or boosting, which can help mitigate the effects of imbalance by focusing on difficult-to-classify examples.

Example: Using SMOTE for Oversampling

Below is a code example demonstrating how to use the imbalanced-learn library to oversample a minority class in a text classification scenario:

python

```python
import pandas as pd

from imblearn.over_sampling import SMOTE

from sklearn.feature_extraction.text import TfidfVectorizer

from sklearn.model_selection import train_test_split


# Example dataset with imbalanced classes
data = {
  "text": [
    "I love this product!",
```

```python
        "This is the worst experience I've had.",

        "Absolutely fantastic!",

        "Not worth the price.",

        "I am very satisfied.",

        "Terrible, would not recommend.",

        "Superb quality and service.",

        "Awful customer support."
    ],
    "label": [1, 0, 1, 0, 1, 0, 1, 0]  # Assume 1 is positive, 0 is negative
}

df = pd.DataFrame(data)


# Artificially create imbalance by reducing minority class samples (for demonstration)

df_majority = df[df['label'] == 1]

df_minority = df[df['label'] == 0].sample(frac=0.5, random_state=42)  # Keep only half of negative samples

df_imbalanced = pd.concat([df_majority, df_minority])


print("Class distribution before SMOTE:")

print(df_imbalanced['label'].value_counts())


# Vectorize text data using TF-IDF

vectorizer = TfidfVectorizer()
```

```python
X = vectorizer.fit_transform(df_imbalanced['text'])

y = df_imbalanced['label']


# Split data into training and test sets

X_train, X_test, y_train, y_test = train_test_split(X, y, test_size=0.2,
random_state=42)


# Apply SMOTE to the training set

smote = SMOTE(random_state=42)

X_train_resampled, y_train_resampled = smote.fit_resample(X_train,
y_train)


print("\nClass distribution after SMOTE:")

print(pd.Series(y_train_resampled).value_counts())
```

Explanation:

- **Data Preparation:**
  A small example dataset is created, and imbalance is simulated by reducing the negative samples.
- **TF-IDF Vectorization:**
  Converts text data into numerical features.
- **SMOTE Application:**
  Oversamples the minority class in the training set, ensuring a balanced class distribution.

Bias Mitigation

Understanding Bias:
Bias in data can emerge from societal prejudices or imbalanced representation of

different groups. For LLMs, this may lead to outputs that are unfair or discriminatory. Bias can be present in the training data or inadvertently amplified by the model.

Strategies for Bias Mitigation:

1. **Data-Level Interventions:**
   - **Diverse Data Collection:** Ensure that your dataset includes a wide range of voices and perspectives.
   - **Annotation Guidelines:** Develop clear guidelines for annotators to reduce subjective bias during labeling.
2. **Algorithm-Level Interventions:**
   - **Debiasing Embeddings:** Techniques such as projecting word embeddings onto a subspace that minimizes gender or racial biases.
   - **Adversarial Training:** Train models with adversarial objectives designed to reduce the influence of biased features.
   - **Fairness Metrics:** Regularly evaluate your model using fairness metrics (e.g., demographic parity, equal opportunity) to quantify and monitor bias.

Example: Evaluating Fairness with a Simple Bias Metric

Below is an example that demonstrates how to evaluate bias using a simple fairness metric. Assume you have a binary classifier and you want to compare the false positive rates (FPR) for two demographic groups.

python

```python
import numpy as np


# Example predictions and true labels for two demographic groups

# Group A and Group B represent two different groups (e.g., based on gender or ethnicity)

true_labels_A = np.array([0, 1, 0, 1, 0])

predictions_A = np.array([0, 1, 1, 1, 0])


true_labels_B = np.array([0, 1, 0, 1, 0])
```

```python
predictions_B = np.array([1, 1, 0, 1, 1])


def false_positive_rate(true_labels, predictions):
    # FP = predicted positive but true label is negative
    false_positives = np.sum((predictions == 1) & (true_labels == 0))
    true_negatives = np.sum(true_labels == 0)
    return false_positives / true_negatives if true_negatives > 0 else 0


fpr_A = false_positive_rate(true_labels_A, predictions_A)
fpr_B = false_positive_rate(true_labels_B, predictions_B)


print("False Positive Rate for Group A:", fpr_A)
print("False Positive Rate for Group B:", fpr_B)


# Calculate disparity in FPR between groups
fpr_disparity = abs(fpr_A - fpr_B)
print("FPR Disparity:", fpr_disparity)
```

Explanation:

- **False Positive Rate Calculation:**
  The function calculates the FPR for each group.
- **Bias Evaluation:**
  The disparity in FPR between groups is computed. A large disparity indicates potential bias that may require mitigation.

4.4 Tools and Pipelines for Efficient Data Management

Efficient data management is essential for scaling machine learning projects, ensuring reproducibility, and streamlining workflows. This section covers tools and pipelines that facilitate efficient data handling, processing, and storage.

Key Tools for Data Management

1. **Hugging Face Datasets Library:**
   - **Purpose:**
   Provides a fast, efficient way to load, process, and share datasets.
   - **Features:**
     - Direct access to thousands of datasets.
     - In-built functions for data transformation, filtering, and splitting.
     - Seamless integration with the Transformers library.
   - **Example Usage:**
   Loading and processing a dataset for fine-tuning a text classification model.
2. **Pandas:**
   - **Purpose:**
   A powerful library for data manipulation and analysis.
   - **Features:**
     - DataFrame structures for handling tabular data.
     - Extensive functions for cleaning, transforming, and aggregating data.
   - **Example Usage:**
   Handling CSV or Excel files containing training data.
3. **Apache Airflow:**
   - **Purpose:**
   An open-source tool for orchestrating complex data workflows.
   - **Features:**
     - Scheduling and managing data pipelines.
     - Monitoring and logging capabilities.
   - **Example Usage:**
   Automating the data ingestion and preprocessing steps in a production environment.
4. **MLflow:**
   - **Purpose:**
   An open-source platform for managing the end-to-end machine learning lifecycle.
   - **Features:**

- Experiment tracking and model versioning.
- Deployment and reproducibility.
  - **Example Usage:**
    Tracking data preprocessing experiments and ensuring reproducibility.

Building a Data Pipeline with Hugging Face Datasets

Below is an example that demonstrates how to create a simple data pipeline using the Hugging Face Datasets library. This pipeline loads a dataset, applies tokenization, and prepares it for model training.

python

```python
from datasets import load_dataset

from transformers import AutoTokenizer


# Load a dataset from the Hugging Face Hub

dataset = load_dataset("ag_news", split="train")


# Define a tokenizer (e.g., for BERT)

tokenizer = AutoTokenizer.from_pretrained("bert-base-uncased")


# Define a tokenization function

def tokenize_function(examples):

    return tokenizer(examples["text"], padding="max_length",
truncation=True, max_length=128)


# Apply the tokenization function to the entire dataset

tokenized_dataset = dataset.map(tokenize_function, batched=True)
```

```
# Display a sample of the tokenized dataset

print(tokenized_dataset[0])
```

Explanation:

- **Dataset Loading:**
  The load_dataset function fetches the AG News dataset.
- **Tokenizer Definition:**
  A pre-trained tokenizer is loaded to convert raw text into tokens.
- **Mapping the Function:**
  The map method applies the tokenization function across all examples, ensuring uniform processing.
- **Output Sample:**
  Printing the first tokenized example verifies the transformation.

Managing Data Pipelines with Apache Airflow

For larger projects, orchestrating your data workflows using tools like Apache Airflow can be highly beneficial. Airflow allows you to schedule tasks, monitor their execution, and ensure that data processing is reproducible and scalable. A typical Airflow DAG (Directed Acyclic Graph) might include tasks for:

- Data ingestion from various sources.
- Data cleaning and preprocessing.
- Tokenization and augmentation.
- Uploading processed data to a central repository or database.

While a full Airflow DAG example is beyond this section's scope, here's a conceptual outline:

Task	Description	Tool/Library

Data Ingestion	Collect raw data from multiple sources	Python scripts, APIs
Data Cleaning	Remove noise, standardize text	Pandas, Regex
Tokenization	Convert text into tokens for model input	Hugging Face Tokenizers
Data Augmentation	Apply synonym replacement, back-translation, etc.	nlpaug, custom scripts
Data Storage & Retrieval	Store processed data in databases or cloud storage	SQL/NoSQL, S3

Handling imbalanced data and mitigating bias are essential for developing fair and effective models. Strategies such as resampling, class weighting, and fairness evaluation help address these challenges, while tools like SMOTE and bias metrics provide practical solutions. Additionally, leveraging modern tools and pipelines—such as the Hugging Face Datasets library, Pandas, Apache Airflow, and MLflow—ensures efficient and reproducible data management. By adopting these practices and tools, you can build a robust data processing pipeline that lays a solid foundation for successful model training and deployment.

Chapter 5: Diving into PyTorch for LLMs

PyTorch is a widely used deep learning framework that provides the flexibility and efficiency required for training large language models (LLMs). In this chapter, we will explore the fundamentals of PyTorch for model training and then discuss how to create custom model architectures tailored for language tasks. The content is presented in a clear, step-by-step manner with code examples, tables, and thorough explanations.

5.1 PyTorch Fundamentals for Model Training

Understanding PyTorch's core concepts is essential for building, training, and fine-tuning models. This section covers the basics of PyTorch, including tensors, automatic differentiation, the data loading pipeline, and the training loop.

At the heart of PyTorch are tensors—multidimensional arrays similar to NumPy arrays but with additional capabilities such as GPU acceleration and automatic differentiation.

Key Concepts:

- **Creation:** You can create tensors from Python lists, NumPy arrays, or directly using PyTorch functions.
- **Operations:** Tensors support a wide range of operations such as addition, multiplication, and matrix operations.
- **Device Management:** Tensors can reside on either the CPU or GPU, enabling faster computation with CUDA-enabled GPUs.

Example: Creating and Manipulating Tensors

python

```python
import torch

# Create a tensor from a Python list
tensor_a = torch.tensor([1, 2, 3])

print("Tensor A:", tensor_a)
```

```python
# Create a random tensor of shape (3, 3)

tensor_b = torch.rand(3, 3)

print("Tensor B:\n", tensor_b)


# Basic operations: addition and multiplication

tensor_sum = tensor_a + 5  # Adds 5 to each element

tensor_product = tensor_a * 2  # Multiplies each element by 2

print("Tensor A + 5:", tensor_sum)

print("Tensor A * 2:", tensor_product)
```

One of PyTorch's most powerful features is its automatic differentiation engine, Autograd. Autograd allows you to compute gradients automatically, which is essential for training neural networks.

Key Concepts:

- **Gradient Tracking:** By setting requires_grad=True, PyTorch tracks operations on a tensor so that gradients can be computed during backpropagation.
- **Backward Propagation:** The .backward() method computes the gradient of the loss with respect to the tensor.

Example: Gradient Computation

python

```python
# Create a tensor and enable gradient tracking

x = torch.tensor([2.0, 3.0], requires_grad=True)
```

```python
# Define a simple function: y = x^2

y = x ** 2

# Compute the sum of the outputs

z = y.sum()


# Compute gradients

z.backward()


# Gradients of z with respect to x (dz/dx = 2*x)

print("Gradients of x:", x.grad)
```

Efficient data handling is crucial for training models. PyTorch provides the torch.utils.data module, which includes classes such as Dataset and DataLoader for managing data pipelines.

Key Concepts:

- **Custom Datasets:** Create a custom Dataset class by implementing the __len__ and __getitem__ methods.
- **DataLoader:** Provides batching, shuffling, and parallel data loading to improve training efficiency.

Example: Custom Dataset and DataLoader

python

```python
from torch.utils.data import Dataset, DataLoader


# Define a custom dataset for demonstration

class TextDataset(Dataset):
```

```python
def __init__(self, texts, labels, tokenizer, max_length=128):
    self.texts = texts
    self.labels = labels
    self.tokenizer = tokenizer
    self.max_length = max_length


def __len__(self):
    return len(self.texts)


def __getitem__(self, idx):
    # Tokenize the text at the given index
    encoding = self.tokenizer(
        self.texts[idx],
        padding='max_length',
        truncation=True,
        max_length=self.max_length,
        return_tensors='pt'
    )
    # Squeeze to remove extra dimensions and return as dictionary
    item = {key: val.squeeze(0) for key, val in encoding.items()}
    item['labels'] = torch.tensor(self.labels[idx], dtype=torch.long)
    return item
```

```python
# Example usage with a dummy tokenizer (assuming a Hugging Face
tokenizer is used)

from transformers import AutoTokenizer

tokenizer = AutoTokenizer.from_pretrained("bert-base-uncased")


texts = ["Hello, world!", "PyTorch is powerful."]

labels = [0, 1]


# Create dataset and DataLoader

dataset = TextDataset(texts, labels, tokenizer)

data_loader = DataLoader(dataset, batch_size=2, shuffle=True)


# Iterate over DataLoader

for batch in data_loader:

    print("Batch input_ids:", batch["input_ids"])

    print("Batch labels:", batch["labels"])
```

The training loop is where the model learns from the data by iteratively adjusting its weights. A typical training loop includes forward propagation, loss computation, backpropagation, and parameter updates.

Key Components:

- **Forward Pass:** Compute model predictions.
- **Loss Function:** Quantifies the difference between predictions and true labels.
- **Backward Pass:** Computes gradients via backpropagation.
- **Optimizer Step:** Updates model parameters.

Example: Simple Training Loop

python

```python
import torch.nn as nn
import torch.optim as optim

# Define a simple model (e.g., a feedforward network)
class SimpleModel(nn.Module):
    def __init__(self, input_size, hidden_size, output_size):
        super(SimpleModel, self).__init__()
        self.fc1 = nn.Linear(input_size, hidden_size)
        self.relu = nn.ReLU()
        self.fc2 = nn.Linear(hidden_size, output_size)

    def forward(self, x):
        out = self.fc1(x)
        out = self.relu(out)
        out = self.fc2(out)
        return out

# Initialize model, loss function, and optimizer
model = SimpleModel(input_size=10, hidden_size=5, output_size=2)
criterion = nn.CrossEntropyLoss()
optimizer = optim.Adam(model.parameters(), lr=0.001)
```

```python
# Dummy input and target tensors

inputs = torch.randn(16, 10)  # Batch of 16 samples, each with 10 features

targets = torch.randint(0, 2, (16,))  # Random binary labels


# Training loop (one epoch)

for epoch in range(5):

    optimizer.zero_grad()       # Clear gradients

    outputs = model(inputs)       # Forward pass

    loss = criterion(outputs, targets)  # Compute loss

    loss.backward()           # Backward pass

    optimizer.step()           # Update parameters

    print(f"Epoch {epoch+1}, Loss: {loss.item():.4f}")
```

Explanation:

- **Model Definition:** A simple feedforward network is defined.
- **Loss and Optimizer:** Cross-entropy loss is used for classification, and Adam is chosen for optimization.
- **Training Loop:** Iteratively performs forward and backward passes, updates model parameters, and prints the loss.

5.2 Custom Model Architectures in PyTorch

While pre-built architectures are available, creating custom models allows you to tailor architectures to specific needs. This section demonstrates how to design and implement custom model architectures in PyTorch for language tasks.

Custom architectures can range from modifications of standard models to entirely novel designs. Key considerations include:

- **Task Requirements:** Adapt the architecture based on whether the task is classification, generation, or regression.
- **Layer Selection:** Choose layers (e.g., convolutional, recurrent, transformer, or fully connected) that suit the data and task.
- **Scalability:** Ensure that the model is scalable and can handle large datasets and complex patterns.

Long Short-Term Memory (LSTM) networks are popular for handling sequential data. The following example demonstrates how to build a custom LSTM-based classifier for text data.

Model Architecture:

- **Embedding Layer:** Converts token IDs into dense vectors.
- **LSTM Layer:** Processes the sequential data.
- **Fully Connected Layer:** Maps the LSTM output to class scores.
- **Dropout Layer:** Prevents overfitting by randomly zeroing out elements during training.

Example Code: Custom LSTM Classifier

python

```python
import torch

import torch.nn as nn


class LSTMClassifier(nn.Module):
    def __init__(self, vocab_size, embed_dim, lstm_hidden_dim,
output_size, num_layers=1, dropout=0.5):

        super(LSTMClassifier, self).__init__()

        # Embedding layer: transforms token indices into dense embeddings

        self.embedding = nn.Embedding(vocab_size, embed_dim)
```

```python
        # LSTM layer: processes the embedded tokens sequentially

        self.lstm = nn.LSTM(input_size=embed_dim, hidden_size=lstm_hidden_dim,
                            num_layers=num_layers, batch_first=True, dropout=dropout)


        # Fully connected layer: maps LSTM output to the desired output size

        self.fc = nn.Linear(lstm_hidden_dim, output_size)


        # Dropout layer: reduces overfitting

        self.dropout = nn.Dropout(dropout)


    def forward(self, x):
        # x shape: (batch_size, sequence_length)

        embedded = self.embedding(x)  # (batch_size, sequence_length, embed_dim)

        lstm_out, _ = self.lstm(embedded)  # (batch_size, sequence_length, lstm_hidden_dim)


        # Use the output of the last time step

        last_output = lstm_out[:, -1, :]  # (batch_size, lstm_hidden_dim)

        last_output = self.dropout(last_output)

        logits = self.fc(last_output)  # (batch_size, output_size)

        return logits
```

```python
# Example usage:

vocab_size = 5000      # Example vocabulary size

embed_dim = 128        # Embedding dimension

lstm_hidden_dim = 64   # LSTM hidden state size

output_size = 2        # Number of classes (e.g., binary classification)


# Create an instance of the LSTMClassifier

model = LSTMClassifier(vocab_size, embed_dim, lstm_hidden_dim,
output_size)


# Dummy input: a batch of 16 sequences, each of length 50 (token indices)

dummy_input = torch.randint(0, vocab_size, (16, 50))

logits = model(dummy_input)


print("Input shape:", dummy_input.shape)

print("Output logits shape:", logits.shape)
```

Explanation:

- **Embedding Layer:**
  The nn.Embedding layer converts each token index into a dense vector.
- **LSTM Layer:**
  The LSTM processes the sequence of embeddings and outputs a sequence of hidden states.
- **Selecting the Final Output:**
  The output from the last time step is used as the summary representation for the sequence.

- **Fully Connected Layer and Dropout:**
  The final output is passed through a dropout layer to prevent overfitting and then through a fully connected layer to produce the final logits.

For tasks requiring the latest advancements in language modeling, you might want to build custom transformer components. While the Hugging Face Transformers library provides ready-to-use models, understanding how to implement your own modules can offer deeper insights and customization.

Example: Custom Transformer Encoder Block

Below is a simplified example of a custom transformer encoder block, which incorporates multi-head self-attention, a feed-forward network, and residual connections with layer normalization:

python

```python
import math


class CustomMultiHeadSelfAttention(nn.Module):
    def __init__(self, d_model, num_heads):
        super(CustomMultiHeadSelfAttention, self).__init__()
        assert d_model % num_heads == 0, "d_model must be divisible by num_heads"
        self.d_model = d_model
        self.num_heads = num_heads
        self.d_k = d_model // num_heads

        self.q_linear = nn.Linear(d_model, d_model)
        self.k_linear = nn.Linear(d_model, d_model)
        self.v_linear = nn.Linear(d_model, d_model)
```

```python
        self.out_linear = nn.Linear(d_model, d_model)


    def forward(self, x):

        batch_size, seq_length, _ = x.size()


        # Linear projections

        Q = self.q_linear(x)

        K = self.k_linear(x)

        V = self.v_linear(x)


        # Reshape into multiple heads

        Q = Q.view(batch_size, seq_length, self.num_heads,
self.d_k).transpose(1, 2)

        K = K.view(batch_size, seq_length, self.num_heads,
self.d_k).transpose(1, 2)

        V = V.view(batch_size, seq_length, self.num_heads,
self.d_k).transpose(1, 2)


        # Scaled dot-product attention

        scores = torch.matmul(Q, K.transpose(-2, -1)) / math.sqrt(self.d_k)

        attn_weights = torch.softmax(scores, dim=-1)

        attn_output = torch.matmul(attn_weights, V)


        # Concatenate heads and pass through final linear layer
```

```python
        attn_output = attn_output.transpose(1,
2).contiguous().view(batch_size, seq_length, self.d_model)

        output = self.out_linear(attn_output)

        return output


class CustomTransformerEncoderBlock(nn.Module):
    def __init__(self, d_model, num_heads, d_ff, dropout=0.1):
        super(CustomTransformerEncoderBlock, self).__init__()
        self.attention = CustomMultiHeadSelfAttention(d_model, num_heads)
        self.norm1 = nn.LayerNorm(d_model)
        self.norm2 = nn.LayerNorm(d_model)
        self.ff = nn.Sequential(
            nn.Linear(d_model, d_ff),
            nn.ReLU(),
            nn.Linear(d_ff, d_model)
        )
        self.dropout = nn.Dropout(dropout)

    def forward(self, x):
        # Self-attention with residual connection and normalization
        attn_output = self.attention(x)
        x = self.norm1(x + self.dropout(attn_output))
        # Feed-forward network with residual connection and normalization
        ff_output = self.ff(x)
```

```python
        x = self.norm2(x + self.dropout(ff_output))

        return x


# Example usage of the custom transformer encoder block
batch_size = 2

seq_length = 10

d_model = 32

num_heads = 4

d_ff = 64


# Dummy input tensor (batch_size, sequence_length, d_model)
dummy_input = torch.rand(batch_size, seq_length, d_model)

encoder_block = CustomTransformerEncoderBlock(d_model, num_heads, d_ff)

encoder_output = encoder_block(dummy_input)


print("Input shape:", dummy_input.shape)

print("Encoder output shape:", encoder_output.shape)
```

Explanation:

- **CustomMultiHeadSelfAttention:**
  Implements multi-head self-attention by projecting the input into query, key, and value vectors, splitting into multiple heads, computing scaled dot-product attention, and then concatenating the results.
- **CustomTransformerEncoderBlock:**
  Combines the custom multi-head self-attention with a feed-forward network.

Residual connections and layer normalization are applied after each sub-layer to stabilize training.

- **Usage:**
  A dummy input is passed through the encoder block, and the output shape is verified.

This chapter has provided a comprehensive overview of PyTorch fundamentals for model training and techniques for creating custom model architectures. We explored the essential building blocks—tensors, autograd, data loaders, and training loops—which form the basis of any deep learning project in PyTorch. Then, we demonstrated how to build custom models, including an LSTM-based classifier and custom transformer components, tailored for language tasks.

Armed with these fundamentals and practical examples, you are now well-equipped to dive into more advanced topics in fine-tuning large language models, experiment with various architectures, and optimize models for your specific domain applications.

5.3 Optimizers, Loss Functions, and Learning Rate Schedules

When training deep learning models with PyTorch, selecting the appropriate optimizer, loss function, and learning rate schedule is critical for achieving fast convergence and good generalization. In this section, we will explore these components in detail, explaining their roles, common choices, and how to implement them with practical code examples.

Optimizers

Optimizers are algorithms that update model parameters (weights and biases) based on the gradients computed during backpropagation. They play a key role in minimizing the loss function.

Common Optimizers:

1. **Stochastic Gradient Descent (SGD):**
   - **Description:** Updates parameters using the gradient of the loss function for each mini-batch.
   - **Pros:** Simple and widely used; works well with momentum.
   - **Cons:** May converge slowly or get stuck in local minima.
2. **Adam (Adaptive Moment Estimation):**
   - **Description:** Combines ideas from RMSProp and momentum by maintaining moving averages of both the gradients and their squares.

- ○ **Pros:** Fast convergence and requires less hyperparameter tuning.
- ○ **Cons:** Can sometimes lead to worse generalization compared to SGD.
3. **RMSProp:**
   - ○ **Description:** Maintains a moving average of squared gradients to adjust the learning rate for each parameter.
   - ○ **Pros:** Performs well in non-stationary settings.
   - ○ **Cons:** Not as popular as Adam for many applications.

Example: Using Adam Optimizer

python

```
import torch.optim as optim

# Assuming 'model' is your PyTorch neural network

optimizer = optim.Adam(model.parameters(), lr=0.001)
```

Loss Functions

Loss functions quantify the difference between the model's predictions and the actual target values. They guide the optimizer on how to update the model parameters.

Common Loss Functions:

1. **Cross-Entropy Loss:**
   - ○ **Use Case:** Classification tasks.
   - ○ **Description:** Combines softmax and negative log-likelihood loss.
2. **Mean Squared Error (MSE) Loss:**
   - ○ **Use Case:** Regression tasks.
   - ○ **Description:** Measures the average squared difference between the predicted and actual values.
3. **Binary Cross-Entropy Loss:**
   - ○ **Use Case:** Binary classification.
   - ○ **Description:** Similar to cross-entropy loss but optimized for two classes.

Example: Using Cross-Entropy Loss

python

```
import torch.nn as nn


# For a classification task with multiple classes

criterion = nn.CrossEntropyLoss()
```

Learning Rate Schedules

Learning rate schedules adjust the learning rate during training. A well-chosen schedule can help the model converge more effectively.

Common Learning Rate Schedules:

1. **Step Decay:**
   - **Description:** Reduces the learning rate by a factor every few epochs.
   - **Example:** Decrease the learning rate by 0.1 every 10 epochs.
2. **Exponential Decay:**
   - **Description:** Multiplies the learning rate by a fixed factor after each epoch.
3. **Cosine Annealing:**
   - **Description:** Varies the learning rate following a cosine curve, often combined with warm restarts.
4. **ReduceLROnPlateau:**
   - **Description:** Monitors a metric (e.g., validation loss) and reduces the learning rate when performance stagnates.

Example: Using ReduceLROnPlateau

python

```
from torch.optim.lr_scheduler import ReduceLROnPlateau
```

```
# Assuming 'optimizer' is defined

scheduler = ReduceLROnPlateau(optimizer, mode='min', factor=0.1,
patience=5)


# In your training loop, after validation:

# val_loss is computed on the validation set

scheduler.step(val_loss)
```

Comparative Overview

Below is a table summarizing the key aspects of optimizers, loss functions, and learning rate schedules:

Component	Common Choices	Key Considerations
Optimizers	SGD, Adam, RMSProp	Convergence speed, sensitivity to hyperparameters, generalization
Loss Functions	Cross-Entropy, MSE, Binary Cross-Entropy	Task type (classification vs. regression), output distribution

Learning Rate Schedules	Step Decay, Exponential Decay, Cosine Annealing, ReduceLROnPlateau	Convergence dynamics, adaptability to plateau in performance

5.4 Debugging and Profiling PyTorch Code

Efficient debugging and profiling are essential to optimize model performance and ensure that your PyTorch code runs correctly and efficiently. This section covers common debugging techniques, tools, and best practices for profiling PyTorch code.

Debugging PyTorch Code

Common Debugging Techniques:

1. **Print Statements and Logging:**
   - Use print statements or logging to check the values of tensors, shapes, and intermediate results.
2. **Assertions:**
   - Use assertions to validate tensor dimensions and data types. This helps catch errors early in the computation graph.
3. **Gradient Checking:**
   - Verify that gradients are computed as expected by inspecting .grad attributes after calling backward().
4. **Using PyTorch's Anomaly Detection:**
   - Enable anomaly detection to track down operations that produce NaN or infinite values.

Example: Enabling Anomaly Detection

python

```
import torch

# Enable anomaly detection
```

```python
torch.autograd.set_detect_anomaly(True)

# Example operation that might cause issues
x = torch.tensor([1.0, 2.0, 3.0], requires_grad=True)

y = x ** 2

z = y.sum()

z.backward()


print("Gradients:", x.grad)
```

Explanation:

- **Anomaly Detection:**
  The call to torch.autograd.set_detect_anomaly(True) helps identify the source of issues during backpropagation by providing detailed error messages.

Profiling PyTorch Code

Profiling helps identify performance bottlenecks in your code. PyTorch offers built-in profiling tools, as well as external libraries, to analyze runtime performance.

Built-in PyTorch Profiler:

The PyTorch Profiler can be used to measure the time taken by different operations in your model. It provides a detailed report that can help optimize performance.

Example: Using the PyTorch Profiler

python

```python
import torch
```

```python
import torch.nn as nn

import torch.optim as optim

from torch.profiler import profile, record_function, ProfilerActivity


# Define a simple model for demonstration
class SimpleModel(nn.Module):
    def __init__(self):
        super(SimpleModel, self).__init__()
        self.fc = nn.Linear(1000, 1000)

    def forward(self, x):
        with record_function("linear_layer"):
            x = self.fc(x)
        return x


model = SimpleModel()

optimizer = optim.Adam(model.parameters(), lr=0.001)

dummy_input = torch.randn(10, 1000)


# Use the profiler to analyze the forward and backward passes
with profile(activities=[ProfilerActivity.CPU], record_shapes=True) as prof:
    output = model(dummy_input)

    loss = output.sum()
```

```
loss.backward()

optimizer.step()
```

```
print(prof.key_averages().table(sort_by="cpu_time_total",
row_limit=10))
```

Explanation:

- **Profiler Context Manager:**
  The profile context manager captures performance metrics for operations
  executed within its block.
- **Record Function:**
  The record_function context helps tag specific sections of code for easier
  identification in the profiler report.
- **Output:**
  The profiler prints a table of key statistics (e.g., total CPU time) for each
  operation, allowing you to pinpoint bottlenecks.

Best Practices for Debugging and Profiling:

- **Modularize Code:**
  Break your code into smaller functions or modules to simplify debugging and
  isolate performance issues.
- **Run on Small Data:**
  Debug on a small subset of data before scaling up to avoid long runtimes during
  testing.
- **Use Version Control:**
  Maintain version control for your code so that you can revert to previous versions
  if new changes introduce bugs.
- **Leverage Visualization:**
  Tools like TensorBoard (with PyTorch support) can help visualize training
  metrics and model architecture, aiding both debugging and performance tuning.

Optimizers, loss functions, and learning rate schedules are the core components that
influence the convergence and generalization of deep learning models. Selecting the
appropriate configurations and tuning them based on the task at hand can lead to
significant performance improvements. Simultaneously, effective debugging and

profiling are indispensable for maintaining code quality and ensuring efficient execution of your PyTorch programs.

By combining best practices with powerful tools like PyTorch's anomaly detection and profiling utilities, you can streamline the development process, rapidly identify issues, and optimize your models for real-world deployment. With these skills, you are better equipped to manage the complexities of training large language models and refining them for specific applications.

Chapter 6: Leveraging Hugging Face for Fine-Tuning

The Hugging Face ecosystem has become synonymous with state-of-the-art natural language processing (NLP) due to its comprehensive suite of tools, models, and libraries. This chapter explains how to leverage the Hugging Face ecosystem for fine-tuning large language models (LLMs). We will begin by introducing the core Transformers library, which provides an easy-to-use interface for a wide array of pre-trained models, and then discuss methods for loading and customizing these models to suit specific tasks.

6.1 Introduction to the Transformers Library

The Transformers library, developed by Hugging Face, is a powerful, open-source framework that offers access to thousands of pre-trained models. These models include BERT, GPT, T5, RoBERTa, and many others, which have been trained on vast amounts of data and are readily adaptable to various NLP tasks such as text classification, question answering, text generation, and more.

Key Features of the Transformers Library

- **Unified API:**
  The library provides a consistent API for loading, fine-tuning, and deploying transformer-based models. The same methods work across different architectures, which streamlines experimentation and integration.
- **Pre-Trained Models:**
  Hundreds of pre-trained models are available through the Hugging Face Model Hub. These models can be easily loaded using the from_pretrained() method, saving significant training time and computational resources.
- **Task-Specific Pipelines:**
  High-level pipelines are available for common tasks such as sentiment analysis, summarization, and translation. These pipelines abstract away the complexity of preprocessing and model inference.
- **Integration with PyTorch and TensorFlow:**
  Although many examples use PyTorch, the Transformers library is compatible with both PyTorch and TensorFlow, making it flexible for various development preferences.
- **Extensive Documentation and Community Support:**
  Hugging Face provides detailed documentation, tutorials, and community

forums, making it easier for developers at all levels to get started and troubleshoot issues.

Table: Key Components of the Transformers Library

Component	Description	Example Use Cases
Model Classes	Pre-trained model architectures (e.g., BertModel, GPT2Model)	Text embeddings, generation, classification
Tokenizer Classes	Tools for converting raw text into token IDs (e.g., BertTokenizer)	Preprocessing input for models
Pipelines	High-level APIs for common tasks (e.g., sentiment analysis, QA)	Quick prototyping for NLP applications
Configuration Files	Files that specify model parameters and hyperparameters	Reproducing and customizing models
Trainer API	High-level API to train and fine-tune models with minimal boilerplate	Fine-tuning on custom datasets

Code Example: Using a High-Level Pipeline

Below is an example of how to use a sentiment analysis pipeline with a pre-trained model:

python

```python
from transformers import pipeline

# Create a sentiment analysis pipeline using a pre-trained model
sentiment_pipeline = pipeline("sentiment-analysis")

# Define some example text
example_text = "I absolutely loved the new update, it's fantastic!"

# Use the pipeline to analyze the sentiment
result = sentiment_pipeline(example_text)

print("Sentiment Analysis Result:")
print(result)
```

Explanation:

- **Pipeline Creation:**
  The pipeline function automatically loads a pre-trained model suitable for the specified task (here, sentiment analysis).
- **Inference:**
  The example text is passed to the pipeline, which returns a sentiment label along with a confidence score.

- **Simplicity:**
  This high-level interface hides the complexities of tokenization, model loading, and inference, making it ideal for quick experimentation.

6.2 Loading and Customizing Pre-Trained Models

While pipelines are excellent for rapid prototyping, fine-tuning and customizing models often require more granular control. In this section, we will discuss how to load pre-trained models and then customize them to suit specific tasks. This process typically involves altering the model's architecture or training regimen to better fit your domain-specific data.

Loading Pre-Trained Models

The Transformers library makes it straightforward to load a pre-trained model using the from_pretrained() method. This method retrieves the model weights and configuration from the Hugging Face Model Hub.

Example: Loading a Pre-Trained BERT Model

python

```python
from transformers import AutoTokenizer,
AutoModelForSequenceClassification


# Specify the pre-trained model name (e.g., BERT for sequence
classification)

model_name = "bert-base-uncased"


# Load the tokenizer and model

tokenizer = AutoTokenizer.from_pretrained(model_name)
```

```python
model =
AutoModelForSequenceClassification.from_pretrained(model_name,
num_labels=2)
```

```python
print("Model loaded successfully!")
```

Explanation:

- **Tokenizer and Model:**
  The code loads both the tokenizer and model for BERT. The tokenizer converts text into numerical tokens, while the model is pre-trained on large corpora.
- **Model Customization Parameter:**
  In this example, num_labels=2 is set for binary classification tasks, indicating that the model's classification head should be adjusted accordingly.

Customizing Pre-Trained Models

Customizing a pre-trained model generally involves modifying the model's head or adding additional layers to capture domain-specific patterns. Fine-tuning is performed on a curated dataset, and the model's weights are updated to optimize performance on the target task.

Modifying the Model Head

For many tasks, only the final classification or regression head of the model needs to be adjusted. This allows you to leverage the general language understanding from the pre-trained model while adapting it to your specific needs.

Example: Customizing the Classification Head

python

```python
import torch.nn as nn
```

```python
from transformers import AutoModel
```

```python
class CustomBERTClassifier(nn.Module):
```

```python
    def __init__(self, model_name, num_labels):

        super(CustomBERTClassifier, self).__init__()

        # Load the pre-trained BERT model without the classification head

        self.bert = AutoModel.from_pretrained(model_name)

        # Add a custom classification head

        self.classifier = nn.Linear(self.bert.config.hidden_size, num_labels)


    def forward(self, input_ids, attention_mask):

        # Get the outputs from BERT (we only need the pooled output)

        outputs = self.bert(input_ids=input_ids,
attention_mask=attention_mask)

        pooled_output = outputs[1]  # pooled_output is typically the second
element

        # Apply the classification head

        logits = self.classifier(pooled_output)

        return logits


# Instantiate the custom classifier

custom_model = CustomBERTClassifier(model_name="bert-base-
uncased", num_labels=2)

print("Custom model architecture created.")
```

Explanation:

- **Model Base:**
  The pre-trained BERT model is loaded without its classification head.

- **Custom Head:**
  A new linear layer is defined to serve as the classification head. The input dimension of this layer is the hidden size of the BERT model.
- **Forward Method:**
  The forward method processes inputs through BERT and then passes the pooled output (typically representing the entire sequence) to the classification head.

Fine-Tuning the Customized Model

Fine-tuning involves training the customized model on your domain-specific dataset. The process is similar to standard training but often requires a lower learning rate to avoid distorting the pre-trained weights.

Example: Fine-Tuning Setup

python

```python
from transformers import Trainer, TrainingArguments


# Assume you have a custom dataset prepared as a Hugging Face Dataset object

# For demonstration, let's assume 'train_dataset' and 'val_dataset' are available


# Define training arguments
training_args = TrainingArguments(

    output_dir="./custom_model_output",

    num_train_epochs=3,

    per_device_train_batch_size=16,

    per_device_eval_batch_size=16,

    evaluation_strategy="epoch",
```

```
    learning_rate=2e-5,

    weight_decay=0.01,

    logging_steps=50,

)


# Initialize the Trainer with the custom model, training arguments, and datasets

trainer = Trainer(

    model=custom_model,

    args=training_args,

    train_dataset=train_dataset,

    eval_dataset=val_dataset,

)


# Start fine-tuning

trainer.train()
```

Explanation:

- **TrainingArguments:**
  These specify hyperparameters such as learning rate, batch size, number of epochs, and output directory.
- **Trainer API:**
  The Trainer class encapsulates the training loop, evaluation, and logging, making it easier to fine-tune the model without writing boilerplate code.
- **Fine-Tuning Process:**
  The call to trainer.train() updates the model weights based on your domain-specific data.

Summary Table: Steps to Load and Customize Pre-Trained Models

Step	Action	Key Functions/Classes
Loading a Pre-Trained Model	Retrieve model and tokenizer from the Model Hub	AutoTokenizer.from _pretrained(), AutoModelForSequenceClassification.from_pretrained()
Customizing the Model Head	Modify the final layer(s) to suit the target task	Custom nn.Module classes, nn.Linear()
Defining the Forward Pass	Combine base model outputs with the custom head	Overridden forward() method
Fine-Tuning Setup	Set training hyperparameters and initiate training	TrainingArguments, Trainer

Leveraging the Hugging Face Transformers library offers a streamlined, powerful approach to fine-tuning large language models. In this chapter, we explored the core features of the Transformers library, including its unified API, access to pre-trained models, and high-level pipelines. We then demonstrated how to load a pre-trained model, customize its architecture for domain-specific tasks, and set up fine-tuning using the Trainer API.

By understanding these processes, you can quickly adapt and optimize pre-trained models for a wide variety of NLP tasks, harnessing the cutting-edge capabilities of transformer architectures while significantly reducing development time and computational requirements.

6.3 Tokenizers and Data Collation Strategies

Tokenization and data collation are critical steps in preparing text data for model training and fine-tuning. In the Hugging Face ecosystem, these processes are highly optimized and customizable, ensuring that raw text is efficiently transformed into a format that models can understand. In this section, we will explore the role of tokenizers, explain various tokenization techniques, and detail strategies for collating data into batches suitable for model training.

The Role of Tokenizers

Tokenizers convert raw text into numerical representations that neural networks can process. They break text down into smaller units—tokens—which can be words, subwords, or even characters. The choice of tokenization strategy affects both the vocabulary size and the model's ability to handle out-of-vocabulary words.

Key Aspects of Tokenization:

- **Vocabulary Construction:**
  Tokenizers build a vocabulary from the training data. Common methods include WordPiece (used by BERT) and Byte-Pair Encoding (BPE, used by GPT-2).
- **Handling Unknown Words:**
  Subword tokenization allows the model to split rare or unknown words into known subword units, improving robustness.
- **Special Tokens:**
  Tokenizers also add special tokens (such as [CLS], [SEP], or <PAD>) to indicate sentence boundaries, classification signals, and padding.

Hugging Face Tokenizers Library

The Hugging Face Tokenizers library is written in Rust for high performance and provides Python bindings. It supports various tokenization methods and is optimized for speed, making it ideal for large-scale NLP applications.

Example: Loading and Using a Tokenizer

Below is an example using the AutoTokenizer class to load a pre-trained tokenizer and apply it to a batch of texts.

python

```python
from transformers import AutoTokenizer

# Load a pre-trained tokenizer (e.g., BERT tokenizer)
tokenizer = AutoTokenizer.from_pretrained("bert-base-uncased")

# Sample texts for tokenization
texts = [
    "Hello, how are you?",
    "Transformers make NLP easier."
]

# Tokenize texts with padding and truncation
encoded_inputs = tokenizer(
    texts,
    padding='max_length',
    truncation=True,
    max_length=16,
    return_tensors="pt"
)

print("Input IDs:")
print(encoded_inputs['input_ids'])
```

```python
print("Attention Masks:")

print(encoded_inputs['attention_mask'])
```

Explanation:

- **Loading the Tokenizer:**
  The AutoTokenizer.from_pretrained method automatically retrieves the tokenizer configuration and vocabulary from the model hub.
- **Padding and Truncation:**
  The parameters padding='max_length' and truncation=True ensure that all sequences are of a uniform length (16 tokens in this case).
- **Returning Tensors:**
  The return_tensors="pt" option converts the tokenized outputs into PyTorch tensors.

Data Collation Strategies

Data collation is the process of assembling individual samples into batches for training. Efficient collation ensures that each batch is uniformly shaped and that padding is appropriately handled.

Key Strategies:

- **Dynamic Padding:**
  Instead of padding every sequence to a fixed maximum length across the entire dataset, dynamic padding pads sequences in each batch to the maximum length found in that batch. This reduces unnecessary computation and memory usage.
- **Custom Collation Functions:**
  When working with complex datasets (e.g., multiple inputs per sample), you can define a custom collation function to process the data before batching.

Example: Custom Collation Function with PyTorch DataLoader

Below is an example of a custom collation function that dynamically pads tokenized sequences:

python

```python
import torch

from torch.nn.utils.rnn import pad_sequence


def custom_collate_fn(batch):
    # Extract input_ids and attention_mask from each sample in the batch
    input_ids_list = [sample['input_ids'] for sample in batch]

    attention_mask_list = [sample['attention_mask'] for sample in batch]

    labels = torch.tensor([sample['labels'] for sample in batch])


    # Dynamically pad the input_ids and attention_mask
    padded_input_ids = pad_sequence(input_ids_list, batch_first=True, padding_value=tokenizer.pad_token_id)

    padded_attention_mask = pad_sequence(attention_mask_list, batch_first=True, padding_value=0)


    return {
        "input_ids": padded_input_ids,

        "attention_mask": padded_attention_mask,

        "labels": labels
    }


# Example usage in a DataLoader
from torch.utils.data import DataLoader
```

```python
# Assume 'dataset' is a Hugging Face Dataset already tokenized and
formatted

data_loader = DataLoader(dataset, batch_size=8,
collate_fn=custom_collate_fn)


# Iterate over the DataLoader and print batch shapes

for batch in data_loader:

    print("Batch input_ids shape:", batch["input_ids"].shape)

    print("Batch attention_mask shape:", batch["attention_mask"].shape)

    print("Batch labels shape:", batch["labels"].shape)

    break
```

Explanation:

- **pad_sequence Function:**
  The pad_sequence utility from PyTorch pads a list of variable-length tensors to a uniform length.
- **Custom Collation:**
  The custom collation function aggregates data samples and pads them on the fly, ensuring efficient batching.
- **Batch Output:**
  The function returns a dictionary containing padded tensors for input_ids, attention_mask, and labels, ready for model input.

6.4 Hugging Face Datasets and Community Contributions

The Hugging Face Datasets library and the broader community contributions are key components of the Hugging Face ecosystem, enabling efficient dataset handling and fostering a collaborative environment for NLP research and development.

Hugging Face Datasets Library

The Datasets library is designed to simplify the process of loading, preprocessing, and sharing datasets. It offers several advantages:

- **Wide Range of Datasets:**
  Access thousands of datasets across various domains directly from the Hugging Face Hub.
- **Efficient Data Loading:**
  Datasets are optimized for memory and speed, supporting streaming, caching, and multiprocessing.
- **Built-In Preprocessing Functions:**
  The library provides functions for mapping, filtering, and transforming datasets, making it easy to integrate tokenization and data augmentation into your workflow.

Example: Loading and Processing a Dataset

Below is an example of how to load the AG News dataset and apply tokenization using the Hugging Face Datasets library.

python

```python
from datasets import load_dataset

from transformers import AutoTokenizer


# Load the AG News dataset

dataset = load_dataset("ag_news", split="train")


# Load a pre-trained tokenizer

tokenizer = AutoTokenizer.from_pretrained("bert-base-uncased")


# Define a tokenization function
```

```python
def tokenize_function(examples):

    return tokenizer(examples["text"], padding="max_length",
truncation=True, max_length=128)


# Apply the tokenization function to the dataset

tokenized_dataset = dataset.map(tokenize_function, batched=True)


print("Sample tokenized example:")

print(tokenized_dataset[0])
```

Explanation:

- **Dataset Loading:**
  The load_dataset function retrieves the AG News dataset from the Hugging Face Hub.
- **Mapping Function:**
  The map method applies the tokenization function to every example in the dataset, processing data in batches for efficiency.
- **Output:**
  A tokenized dataset is produced, where each example now contains numerical representations ready for model training.

Community Contributions

Hugging Face thrives on a vibrant community of researchers, developers, and enthusiasts who contribute to its libraries, share pre-trained models, and publish datasets. These contributions have several benefits:

- **Model Sharing:**
  Users can upload and share models on the Hugging Face Model Hub, facilitating collaboration and accelerating innovation.

- **Dataset Contributions:**
  Researchers can contribute datasets that are annotated, cleaned, and curated, making them available for a global audience.
- **Tutorials and Notebooks:**
  Community-driven tutorials and example notebooks provide practical insights into how to use Hugging Face tools effectively.

Table: Benefits of Community Contributions

Aspect	Benefit
Model Hub	Access to a wide range of pre-trained models and fine-tuning examples.
Datasets Library	Availability of diverse and well-curated datasets for various tasks.
Tutorials and Documentation	Detailed guides, tutorials, and code examples shared by the community.
Collaboration and Feedback	An active forum for discussing issues, sharing improvements, and staying updated with the latest research.

Best Practices for Leveraging Community Contributions

- **Stay Updated:**
  Regularly check the Hugging Face Model Hub and Datasets repository for new contributions and updates.

- **Engage with the Community:**
  Participate in forums, GitHub discussions, and social media channels to share your experiences and learn from others.
- **Contribute Back:**
  If you develop a useful dataset, model, or tool, consider contributing it back to the community. This fosters collaboration and enhances the ecosystem for everyone.

In this section, we explored the essential role of tokenizers in transforming raw text into model-ready inputs, and we discussed effective data collation strategies to ensure that batches are efficiently formed for training. We then delved into the Hugging Face Datasets library, which provides streamlined access to a wide range of datasets, and highlighted the significant impact of community contributions in enhancing and maintaining the ecosystem.

By mastering tokenization, collation, and data management with Hugging Face tools, you can streamline your data preparation process and focus on fine-tuning models for your specific tasks. This strong foundation not only speeds up experimentation but also leverages the collective expertise of a thriving global community.

Chapter 7: Core Principles of Fine-Tuning

Fine-tuning is the process of adapting a pre-trained model to a specific task or domain by training it further on a smaller, specialized dataset. This chapter delves into the core principles that underlie effective fine-tuning. We will first explore the concept of model adaptation, explaining why and how a general-purpose model is transformed into a task-specific tool. Then, we will examine supervised fine-tuning techniques, which are the most common approach to achieve this transformation.

7.1 Understanding Model Adaptation

Overview

Pre-trained models are built on large, diverse datasets to develop a broad understanding of language. However, these models are typically generalists—they perform well on a variety of tasks but may not excel in a specific application. Model adaptation, or fine-tuning, is the process of adjusting these models to better meet the demands of a particular task or domain.

Why Model Adaptation is Necessary

- **Domain Specificity:**
  Pre-trained models might not capture the unique vocabulary, style, or context-specific information present in specialized domains such as legal, medical, or technical fields. Adaptation helps the model learn these nuances.
- **Task-Specific Performance:**
  While a model like BERT can understand general language, it may require additional training to excel at specific tasks such as sentiment analysis, question answering, or named entity recognition. Fine-tuning aligns the model's predictions with the requirements of the target task.
- **Resource Efficiency:**
  Training large language models from scratch requires extensive computational resources and time. Fine-tuning leverages the general knowledge already learned during pre-training, requiring only a fraction of the data and computational power to achieve high performance on specific tasks.

How Model Adaptation Works

1. **Initialization with Pre-Trained Weights:**
   The process begins with a pre-trained model that has been exposed to vast amounts of text data. This model has already learned general language patterns.
2. **Task-Specific Head Replacement or Addition:**
   Often, the final layer (or "head") of the model is replaced or modified to suit the specific task. For example, in classification tasks, the original head is replaced with a classification layer that outputs class probabilities.
3. **Training on a Specialized Dataset:**
   The model is then further trained (fine-tuned) on a smaller, labeled dataset that is specific to the target task. During this stage, the model's parameters are adjusted so that it learns to map inputs to the desired outputs accurately.
4. **Regularization and Lower Learning Rates:**
   Fine-tuning typically involves a lower learning rate than training from scratch, ensuring that the pre-trained knowledge is not overwritten too quickly. Regularization techniques (such as dropout) are also employed to prevent overfitting on the smaller dataset.

Visual Summary: Model Adaptation Process

Step	Description
Pre-Trained Model	A model trained on a large, diverse corpus that understands general language patterns.
Task-Specific Head Modification	Replace or adjust the final layer(s) to suit the target task (e.g., classification, regression).
Fine-Tuning	Train on a specialized dataset with a lower learning rate and regularization to adapt the model.

Result	A model that retains broad language knowledge but is now optimized for a specific application.

7.2 Supervised Fine-Tuning Techniques

Overview

Supervised fine-tuning is the most widely used approach, where the model is further trained on labeled data for a specific task. This section describes various techniques and best practices for supervised fine-tuning.

Key Techniques in Supervised Fine-Tuning

1. **Data Preparation and Labeling:**
   - **High-Quality Labeled Data:**
     The success of supervised fine-tuning depends on the quality of the labeled dataset. Curated, domain-specific datasets help the model learn task-relevant patterns.
   - **Balanced and Diverse Data:**
     Ensuring that the dataset covers the range of scenarios encountered in the target domain helps the model generalize better.
2. **Freezing and Unfreezing Layers:**
   - **Freezing Early Layers:**
     In some cases, the early layers of a pre-trained model (which capture general features) are frozen (i.e., not updated during training) to preserve the learned representations. This allows the model to focus on adapting the later layers for task-specific details.
   - **Gradual Unfreezing:**
     Alternatively, a gradual unfreezing strategy can be employed, where layers are unfrozen one by one as training progresses. This controlled adaptation can prevent drastic changes to the pre-trained weights.
3. **Learning Rate Scheduling:**
   - **Lower Learning Rates:**
     Using a smaller learning rate during fine-tuning ensures that the pre-trained weights are adjusted gently, preserving the general knowledge while still learning task-specific patterns.

- ○ **Learning Rate Warmup:**
  A warmup period where the learning rate is gradually increased at the beginning of training can help stabilize the fine-tuning process.
4. **Regularization Techniques:**
   - ○ **Dropout:**
     Dropout is often applied to prevent overfitting, especially when fine-tuning on small datasets.
   - ○ **Weight Decay:**
     Adding weight decay (L2 regularization) can also help in controlling overfitting by penalizing large weight updates.

Example: Supervised Fine-Tuning for Text Classification

Below is a complete example demonstrating how to fine-tune a pre-trained BERT model for a binary text classification task using the Hugging Face Transformers library and PyTorch.

Step 1: Setup and Data Preparation

python

```python
from transformers import AutoTokenizer, AutoModelForSequenceClassification, Trainer, TrainingArguments

from datasets import load_dataset


# Load a pre-trained tokenizer and model for classification

model_name = "bert-base-uncased"

tokenizer = AutoTokenizer.from_pretrained(model_name)

model = AutoModelForSequenceClassification.from_pretrained(model_name, num_labels=2)


# Load a sample dataset (using the 'imdb' dataset for sentiment analysis as an example)
```

```python
dataset = load_dataset("imdb")

# For demonstration, we use a small subset

train_dataset = dataset["train"].shuffle(seed=42).select(range(2000))

test_dataset = dataset["test"].shuffle(seed=42).select(range(500))


# Define a tokenization function

def tokenize_function(examples):

    return tokenizer(examples["text"], padding="max_length",
truncation=True, max_length=128)


# Apply the tokenization function to the datasets

train_dataset = train_dataset.map(tokenize_function, batched=True)

test_dataset = test_dataset.map(tokenize_function, batched=True)
```

Step 2: Configuring Training Arguments and Fine-Tuning

python

```python
# Define training arguments

training_args = TrainingArguments(

    output_dir="./fine_tuned_bert",

    num_train_epochs=3,

    per_device_train_batch_size=16,

    per_device_eval_batch_size=16,

    evaluation_strategy="epoch",
```

```python
    learning_rate=2e-5,

    weight_decay=0.01,

    logging_steps=50,

    load_best_model_at_end=True,

)


# Initialize the Trainer

trainer = Trainer(

    model=model,

    args=training_args,

    train_dataset=train_dataset,

    eval_dataset=test_dataset,

)


# Start fine-tuning

trainer.train()
```

Explanation:

- **Tokenizer and Model Loading:**
  We load a pre-trained BERT model and its tokenizer, adjusting the classification head for binary classification.
- **Dataset Preparation:**
  The IMDB dataset is used as an example; texts are tokenized with a fixed maximum length, ensuring uniform input size.
- **Training Arguments:**
  We set key parameters such as learning rate, batch sizes, number of epochs, and weight decay. The learning rate is kept low (2e-5) to ensure gentle fine-tuning.

- **Trainer API:**
  The Trainer encapsulates the training loop, evaluation, and logging. The best model is loaded at the end based on evaluation performance.

Summary Table: Supervised Fine-Tuning Techniques

Technique	Description	Benefits
High-Quality Labeled Data	Use curated, domain-specific, balanced, and diverse datasets.	Ensures task-relevant learning and robust performance.
Freezing Layers	Freeze early layers to preserve general features; gradually unfreeze if needed.	Focuses training on task-specific layers; prevents overfitting.
Lower Learning Rates	Use a smaller learning rate during fine-tuning and possibly warmup phases.	Preserves pre-trained knowledge while adapting to new tasks.
Regularization	Employ dropout and weight decay.	Prevents overfitting on smaller datasets.

Fine-tuning through supervised learning is a powerful method for adapting pre-trained models to specific tasks. Understanding model adaptation helps you appreciate how a general-purpose model can be specialized for a particular domain or task. By employing supervised fine-tuning techniques such as careful data preparation, selective layer freezing, controlled learning rate schedules, and regularization, you can significantly enhance the performance of your model on task-specific challenges.

With the comprehensive explanation and detailed code examples provided in this chapter, you are now equipped to implement effective fine-tuning strategies that leverage the strengths of pre-trained models while tailoring them to your specialized needs.

7.3 Reinforcement Learning from Human Feedback (RLHF)

Reinforcement Learning from Human Feedback (RLHF) is an advanced technique used to further refine and optimize language models by incorporating human judgments into the training process. Unlike traditional supervised fine-tuning, which relies solely on labeled data, RLHF leverages human evaluations of model outputs to guide the learning process. This approach is particularly useful when the desired behavior is complex, subjective, or difficult to specify with a standard loss function.

Key Concepts of RLHF

- **Human Feedback:**
  In RLHF, human evaluators provide feedback on the quality of the model's outputs. This feedback is used to generate a reward signal that guides the model's learning. The feedback can be in the form of rankings, ratings, or binary preferences (e.g., "good" vs. "bad").
- **Reward Model:**
  A reward model is trained to predict human preferences based on the outputs of the language model. This model converts qualitative human feedback into a quantitative reward signal that can be optimized via reinforcement learning.
- **Policy Optimization:**
  The language model is treated as a policy that generates outputs. Reinforcement learning algorithms, such as Proximal Policy Optimization (PPO), are used to update the model parameters in order to maximize the expected reward. This process encourages the model to generate outputs that align with human preferences.
- **Iterative Process:**
  RLHF is typically an iterative process where the model is fine-tuned using reinforcement learning, then evaluated, and further refined based on additional human feedback.

Benefits of RLHF

- **Alignment with Human Values:**
  RLHF helps in aligning the model's behavior with human judgments, making its outputs more useful and less prone to errors or biases.
- **Handling Subjectivity:**
  In scenarios where the quality of an output is subjective (e.g., conversational quality or creativity), RLHF can capture nuances that are difficult to quantify using traditional supervised learning.
- **Dynamic Improvement:**
  As more human feedback is collected, the model can continually improve, adapting to new requirements and evolving standards.

RLHF Workflow Overview

Below is a high-level table summarizing the RLHF process:

Step	Description
1. Data Collection	Generate outputs using the pre-trained model and collect human feedback on these outputs.
2. Reward Model Training	Train a reward model that maps model outputs to reward scores based on human feedback.
3. Policy Optimization	Use reinforcement learning (e.g., PPO) to fine-tune the language model, optimizing for higher reward scores.
4. Iteration	Repeat the process by generating new outputs, collecting more

	feedback, and refining the reward model and policy.

Code Example: Pseudocode for RLHF Using PPO

While a full implementation of RLHF can be complex and system-dependent, the following pseudocode outlines the basic structure of applying PPO for RLHF:

python

```python
import torch

from transformers import AutoModelForCausalLM, AutoTokenizer

# Assume a PPO library is available (e.g., from stable-baselines3 or a custom implementation)


# Load pre-trained language model and tokenizer

model_name = "gpt2"

model = AutoModelForCausalLM.from_pretrained(model_name)

tokenizer = AutoTokenizer.from_pretrained(model_name)


# Define a function to generate output given a prompt

def generate_output(prompt, model, tokenizer, max_length=100):

    inputs = tokenizer.encode(prompt, return_tensors="pt")

    outputs = model.generate(inputs, max_length=max_length)

    return tokenizer.decode(outputs[0], skip_special_tokens=True)
```

```python
# Simulated function to obtain human feedback (in practice, this would be
replaced by actual human evaluations)

def get_human_feedback(output):

    # For demonstration, we simulate feedback as a reward value

    # A higher reward means better alignment with human preferences

    return 1.0 if "good" in output.lower() else 0.0


# Pseudocode for training loop using PPO for RLHF

for iteration in range(num_iterations):

    # Generate outputs from the current policy (language model)

    prompt = "Once upon a time"

    generated_output = generate_output(prompt, model, tokenizer)


    # Obtain reward from human feedback (or simulated feedback)

    reward = get_human_feedback(generated_output)


    # Compute the loss and update the model using PPO optimization
(pseudocode)

    # Here, `ppo_step` represents a function from a PPO library that
performs one optimization step.

    loss = ppo_step(model, generated_output, reward)


    # Log training progress

    print(f"Iteration {iteration+1}: Reward = {reward}, Loss = {loss.item()}")
```

Note: This pseudocode is a simplified illustration. Actual RLHF implementations involve additional details

such as computing advantages, maintaining a separate old policy, and clipping in PPO.

Explanation:

- **Model and Tokenizer Loading:**
  A pre-trained GPT-2 model and its tokenizer are loaded.
- **Output Generation:**
  The model generates text based on a given prompt.
- **Simulated Human Feedback:**
  A simple function simulates human feedback by returning a reward score.
- **PPO Training Loop:**
  In each iteration, the model generates outputs, receives a reward, and is updated using a PPO optimization step. Actual RLHF systems include more detailed handling of the reinforcement learning components.

7.4 Evaluating Fine-Tuning Effectiveness

Evaluating the effectiveness of fine-tuning is a critical part of the model development process. It ensures that the adaptations made during fine-tuning lead to improvements in performance, reliability, and alignment with user expectations. Evaluation should be both quantitative and qualitative.

Key Evaluation Metrics

1. **Quantitative Metrics:**
   - **Accuracy, Precision, Recall, F1-Score:**
     Standard metrics for classification tasks. They provide insights into the model's ability to correctly predict labels.
   - **BLEU, ROUGE, METEOR:**
     Metrics for evaluating text generation or summarization tasks. They measure the similarity between generated text and reference text.

- o **Loss Metrics:**
  Training and validation loss values indicate how well the model is learning and can help detect overfitting or underfitting.
- o **Reward Score (for RLHF):**
  When using RLHF, the average reward score from human feedback can serve as a direct indicator of alignment with desired behavior.

2. **Qualitative Metrics:**
   - o **Human Evaluation:**
     Experts or end-users review model outputs to assess quality, coherence, and relevance.
   - o **Case Studies and Error Analysis:**
     Detailed analysis of specific examples where the model performs well or fails. This helps identify areas for further improvement.
   - o **User Satisfaction Surveys:**
     Feedback from users who interact with the model in real-world applications.

Evaluating with Validation Sets and A/B Testing

- **Validation Sets:**
  A dedicated validation set should be used during fine-tuning to monitor performance over time. This helps in adjusting hyperparameters and ensuring that the model is not overfitting.
- **A/B Testing:**
  In production settings, A/B testing can be used to compare the fine-tuned model against the previous version or a baseline model. This method provides real-world evidence of improvements and user satisfaction.

Code Example: Evaluating a Fine-Tuned Classification Model

Below is an example of evaluating a fine-tuned BERT model for a text classification task using the Hugging Face Trainer API and scikit-learn metrics.

python

```
from transformers import AutoTokenizer,
AutoModelForSequenceClassification, Trainer, TrainingArguments
```

```python
from datasets import load_dataset
from sklearn.metrics import accuracy_score,
precision_recall_fscore_support


# Load the fine-tuned model and tokenizer

model_name = "./fine_tuned_bert"

tokenizer = AutoTokenizer.from_pretrained(model_name)

model =
AutoModelForSequenceClassification.from_pretrained(model_name)


# Load the test dataset (using IMDB for sentiment analysis as an example)

dataset = load_dataset("imdb", split="test")
# For demonstration, select a small subset

test_dataset = dataset.shuffle(seed=42).select(range(500))


# Tokenize the test dataset

def tokenize_function(examples):

    return tokenizer(examples["text"], padding="max_length",
truncation=True, max_length=128)


test_dataset = test_dataset.map(tokenize_function, batched=True)


# Define a compute_metrics function for evaluation

def compute_metrics(eval_pred):

    logits, labels = eval_pred
```

```python
    predictions = logits.argmax(axis=-1)

    precision, recall, f1, _ = precision_recall_fscore_support(labels,
predictions, average="binary")

    acc = accuracy_score(labels, predictions)

    return {

        "accuracy": acc,

        "f1": f1,

        "precision": precision,

        "recall": recall,

    }


# Set up Trainer for evaluation (only for evaluation, no training arguments
needed here)
training_args = TrainingArguments(

    output_dir="./results",

    per_device_eval_batch_size=16,

    do_eval=True,

    logging_steps=50,
)


trainer = Trainer(

    model=model,

    args=training_args,

    eval_dataset=test_dataset,
```

```
    compute_metrics=compute_metrics,

)


# Evaluate the model

eval_results = trainer.evaluate()

print("Evaluation Results:", eval_results)
```

Explanation:

- **Model and Tokenizer Loading:**
  The fine-tuned model is loaded from a local directory.
- **Dataset Preparation:**
  The IMDB test dataset is loaded, tokenized, and a subset is selected.
- **Metrics Function:**
  The compute_metrics function computes accuracy, precision, recall, and F1-score using scikit-learn.
- **Evaluation with Trainer:**
  The Trainer's evaluate() method is used to obtain quantitative metrics for the model.

Visual Summary: Evaluation Process

Evaluation Aspect	Approach	Key Tools/Methods
Quantitative Metrics	Use standard metrics for classification, generation, and regression	Accuracy, F1, BLEU, ROUGE, loss curves

Qualitative Evaluation	Gather human judgments, perform error analysis, and conduct user satisfaction surveys	Expert reviews, A/B testing, case studies
Validation Set Monitoring	Regularly assess performance on a dedicated validation set during fine-tuning	Validation loss, early stopping, hyperparameter tuning
A/B Testing	Compare different model versions in real-world settings	User feedback, conversion metrics, engagement rates

Reinforcement Learning from Human Feedback (RLHF) and robust evaluation methodologies play vital roles in the fine-tuning process. RLHF enhances model alignment with human values and subjective quality criteria by integrating human judgment into the training loop through reward models and policy optimization. Meanwhile, evaluating fine-tuning effectiveness through both quantitative metrics and qualitative assessments ensures that the adaptations not only improve task-specific performance but also meet the expectations of end users.

By understanding and implementing these advanced fine-tuning strategies, you can refine large language models to achieve superior, reliable, and ethically-aligned performance in real-world applications.

Chapter 8: Advanced Fine-Tuning Techniques

In this chapter, we delve into advanced techniques that go beyond standard fine-tuning approaches. These methods aim to further optimize model performance and adaptability across various tasks and domains. We cover two major topics: layer-wise learning rate decay with differential training, and strategies for multi-task and multi-domain fine-tuning.

8.1 Layer-Wise Learning Rate Decay and Differential Training

When fine-tuning large language models (LLMs), not all layers require the same degree of adjustment. Pre-trained models have learned useful general representations in early layers that may need only slight modifications, whereas later layers that are more task-specific often benefit from more significant updates. Layer-wise learning rate decay (LLRD) and differential training are techniques that allow for this granular control by applying different learning rates to different layers of the model.

What is Layer-Wise Learning Rate Decay?

Layer-Wise Learning Rate Decay (LLRD) is a technique where each layer of the model is assigned a different learning rate during fine-tuning. Typically, the learning rate is set lower for the earlier layers (closer to the input) and higher for the later layers (closer to the output). This strategy helps preserve the general knowledge learned during pre-training while allowing task-specific layers to adapt more quickly.

Differential Training

Differential Training extends the idea of LLRD by grouping parameters based on their roles or depths within the model. Each group can have its own learning rate and weight decay settings. This approach provides fine-grained control over the training dynamics, reducing the risk of "catastrophic forgetting" (i.e., losing valuable pre-trained knowledge).

Why Use LLRD and Differential Training?

- **Preservation of Pre-Trained Knowledge:**
  Lower learning rates in earlier layers help prevent large weight updates that might disrupt the general language representations.

- **Enhanced Task Adaptation:**
  Higher learning rates in later layers enable the model to more rapidly learn task-specific features.
- **Stability:**
  Differential training can lead to a more stable training process, especially when fine-tuning on small or specialized datasets.

Implementation Example

Below is an example demonstrating how to set up differential learning rates in PyTorch for a pre-trained model using the Hugging Face Transformers library. In this example, we create parameter groups with decayed learning rates for different layers.

python

```python
import torch

from transformers import AutoModelForSequenceClassification, AutoTokenizer


# Load a pre-trained model (e.g., BERT)

model_name = "bert-base-uncased"

model = AutoModelForSequenceClassification.from_pretrained(model_name, num_labels=2)


# Define base learning rate and decay factor

base_lr = 2e-5

layer_decay = 0.95


# Create parameter groups with layer-wise learning rate decay

optimizer_grouped_parameters = []
```

```python
# Assume model.bert.encoder.layer is a list of Transformer layers
for i, layer in enumerate(model.bert.encoder.layer):
    # Calculate decayed learning rate for this layer
    lr = base_lr * (layer_decay ** (len(model.bert.encoder.layer) - i - 1))
    optimizer_grouped_parameters.append({
        "params": layer.parameters(),
        "lr": lr,
    })


# Add remaining parameters (e.g., embedding and classifier layers) with
the base learning rate
optimizer_grouped_parameters.append({
    "params": model.bert.embeddings.parameters(),
    "lr": base_lr * (layer_decay ** len(model.bert.encoder.layer)),
})
optimizer_grouped_parameters.append({
    "params": model.classifier.parameters(),
    "lr": base_lr,
})


# Initialize the optimizer (e.g., AdamW)
from transformers import AdamW
optimizer = AdamW(optimizer_grouped_parameters, lr=base_lr)
```

```
print("Optimized parameter groups with layer-wise learning rate decay:")

for group in optimizer.param_groups:

    print(f"Learning Rate: {group['lr']:.8f}, Number of Params: {len(group['params'])}")
```

Explanation:

- **Base Learning Rate and Decay Factor:**
  A base learning rate is defined, and a decay factor (e.g., 0.95) is applied across layers.
- **Parameter Grouping:**
  We iterate through the transformer layers in the encoder, assigning each layer a decayed learning rate. The embeddings and classifier parameters are grouped separately.
- **Optimizer Initialization:**
  The AdamW optimizer is initialized with these parameter groups, ensuring that each group uses its designated learning rate.

Summary Table: LLRD and Differential Training

Aspect	Description
Early Layers	Lower learning rate to preserve general language features
Later Layers	Higher learning rate for faster adaptation to task-specific patterns
Parameter Grouping	Different parameter groups can have custom learning rates and weight decay settings

Benefits	Improved stability, preservation of pre-trained knowledge, and enhanced task adaptation

8.2 Multi-Task and Multi-Domain Fine-Tuning

Multi-task and multi-domain fine-tuning extend the concept of adaptation by training a single model on multiple tasks or across different domains simultaneously. This approach can improve generalization, reduce the need for separate models, and leverage shared representations across tasks.

Multi-Task Fine-Tuning

Multi-Task Fine-Tuning involves training a model on several tasks at once. Instead of fine-tuning for a single task, the model learns to handle multiple objectives, which may include tasks such as text classification, named entity recognition, and question answering. This is typically achieved by sharing a common encoder (the pre-trained backbone) while using task-specific heads for each task.

Benefits of Multi-Task Fine-Tuning

- **Shared Representations:**
  The model learns robust representations that are useful across different tasks.
- **Data Efficiency:**
  Leveraging data from multiple tasks can help when the dataset for a particular task is limited.
- **Improved Generalization:**
  Multi-task learning often leads to models that generalize better to unseen data.

Multi-Domain Fine-Tuning

Multi-Domain Fine-Tuning is a similar concept but focuses on adapting a model to work across different domains (e.g., legal, medical, financial). The model is trained on data from various domains, either simultaneously or in a sequential manner, to learn domain-invariant features while also capturing domain-specific nuances.

Benefits of Multi-Domain Fine-Tuning

- **Versatility:**
  A single model can serve multiple domains, reducing the need for domain-specific models.
- **Transfer Learning:**
  Knowledge gained from one domain can help improve performance in another, particularly when domains share common language patterns.

Implementation Example: Multi-Task Model with Shared Encoder

Below is an example of a simplified multi-task model in PyTorch that shares a common BERT encoder and uses separate classification heads for two tasks.

python

```python
import torch

import torch.nn as nn

from transformers import AutoModel


class MultiTaskBERT(nn.Module):
    def __init__(self, model_name, num_labels_task1, num_labels_task2):
        super(MultiTaskBERT, self).__init__()
        # Load the shared BERT encoder
        self.bert = AutoModel.from_pretrained(model_name)
        hidden_size = self.bert.config.hidden_size

        # Define task-specific classification heads
        self.classifier_task1 = nn.Linear(hidden_size, num_labels_task1)
        self.classifier_task2 = nn.Linear(hidden_size, num_labels_task2)
```

```python
    def forward(self, input_ids, attention_mask, task="task1"):

        outputs = self.bert(input_ids=input_ids,
attention_mask=attention_mask)

        pooled_output = outputs[1]  # Use the pooled output (CLS token
representation)


        # Select the appropriate classifier based on the task
        if task == "task1":
            logits = self.classifier_task1(pooled_output)
        elif task == "task2":
            logits = self.classifier_task2(pooled_output)
        else:
            raise ValueError("Invalid task identifier provided.")


        return logits


# Example usage:
model_name = "bert-base-uncased"
num_labels_task1 = 3  # e.g., three classes for task 1
num_labels_task2 = 2  # e.g., binary classification for task 2


multi_task_model = MultiTaskBERT(model_name, num_labels_task1,
num_labels_task2)


# Create dummy input tensors
```

```python
dummy_input_ids = torch.randint(0, 30522, (4, 64))  # Batch of 4
sequences, each 64 tokens long

dummy_attention_mask = torch.ones(4, 64)


# Forward pass for task1

logits_task1 = multi_task_model(dummy_input_ids,
dummy_attention_mask, task="task1")

print("Logits for Task 1:", logits_task1.shape)  # Expected shape: (4, 3)


# Forward pass for task2

logits_task2 = multi_task_model(dummy_input_ids,
dummy_attention_mask, task="task2")

print("Logits for Task 2:", logits_task2.shape)  # Expected shape: (4, 2)
```

Explanation:

- **Shared Encoder:**
  The BERT model is loaded as a shared encoder for both tasks.
- **Task-Specific Heads:**
  Two separate linear layers serve as classification heads for the two tasks.
- **Forward Pass:**
  Based on the specified task, the model selects the corresponding head to produce
  logits.
- **Dummy Data:**
  Dummy inputs are provided to simulate a forward pass for each task, and the
  output shapes are printed to verify correctness.

Summary Table: Multi-Task and Multi-Domain Fine-Tuning

Aspect	Description	Benefits

Multi-Task Fine-Tuning	Training one model on multiple tasks with shared encoders and task-specific heads	Shared representations, improved data efficiency, better generalization
Multi-Domain Fine-Tuning	Adapting a model to work across various domains, leveraging both domain-invariant and domain-specific features	Versatility, cross-domain knowledge transfer
Implementation	Can involve separate output heads or multi-task loss functions to handle different tasks	Reduced need for multiple models, streamlined deployment

Advanced fine-tuning techniques such as layer-wise learning rate decay with differential training and multi-task/multi-domain fine-tuning enable a more nuanced and effective adaptation of large language models. By applying different learning rates to different layers, practitioners can preserve valuable pre-trained knowledge while allowing task-specific layers to adapt quickly. Meanwhile, multi-task and multi-domain approaches enable a single model to handle diverse challenges, leading to improved generalization and efficiency.

With the detailed explanations, code examples, and summary tables provided in this chapter, you are now equipped to implement these advanced strategies and further enhance the performance of your models across a variety of applications and domains.

8.3 Incorporating External Knowledge Sources

Incorporating external knowledge sources into large language models (LLMs) can significantly enhance their performance, particularly in tasks that require specialized or up-to-date information. External knowledge can come from various structured and unstructured data sources such as knowledge graphs, databases, or even curated text collections. By integrating this external information, models can generate more informed and contextually rich responses.

Why Incorporate External Knowledge?

- **Enhanced Contextual Understanding:**
  External knowledge provides additional context that can help disambiguate queries and improve the relevance of responses.
- **Filling Knowledge Gaps:**
  Even the most extensive pre-trained models may have gaps, especially with rapidly evolving domains. Supplementing these models with external data keeps them current.
- **Improved Accuracy in Specialized Domains:**
  For technical, medical, legal, or financial applications, domain-specific information from external sources ensures that the model's outputs adhere to the required standards and terminologies.

Methods to Incorporate External Knowledge

1. **Retrieval-Augmented Generation (RAG):**
   This approach combines a retrieval system with a generative model. The retriever searches an external corpus for relevant documents, and the generator conditions its output on both the query and the retrieved documents.
2. **Knowledge Graph Integration:**
   Models can be enhanced by incorporating structured information from knowledge graphs. For example, entity embeddings from a graph can be merged with text embeddings to provide richer context.
3. **Memory Networks:**
   These networks allow models to read from and write to an external memory bank, which can store factual data or long-term knowledge that is updated periodically.
4. **Prompt Engineering with External Data:**
   In some cases, external knowledge is incorporated by designing prompts that include relevant context or factual snippets, guiding the model toward more accurate outputs.

Example: Retrieval-Augmented Generation (RAG) with Hugging Face

Below is an example of setting up a Retrieval-Augmented Generation pipeline using Hugging Face's RAG model. This pipeline retrieves relevant passages from an external dataset and uses them to generate a response.

python

```python
from transformers import RagTokenizer, RagRetriever,
RagTokenForGeneration


# Load the pre-trained RAG tokenizer, retriever, and model

model_name = "facebook/rag-token-nq"

tokenizer = RagTokenizer.from_pretrained(model_name)

retriever = RagRetriever.from_pretrained(model_name,
index_name="exact", use_dummy_dataset=True)

model = RagTokenForGeneration.from_pretrained(model_name,
retriever=retriever)


# Define an input query

query = "What are the latest developments in renewable energy?"


# Tokenize the input and generate a response

input_dict = tokenizer.prepare_seq2seq_batch(query,
return_tensors="pt")

generated_ids = model.generate(input_ids=input_dict["input_ids"],
max_length=100)

generated_text = tokenizer.batch_decode(generated_ids,
skip_special_tokens=True)[0]


print("Generated Response:")

print(generated_text)
```

Explanation:

- **Tokenizer, Retriever, and Model Loading:**
  The RAG model components are loaded from Hugging Face. The retriever is configured to search an external dataset (here a dummy dataset is used for demonstration).
- **Input Preparation:**
  The query is tokenized using prepare_seq2seq_batch, which formats the input appropriately for the RAG model.
- **Generation:**
  The model generates an answer conditioned on both the input query and the retrieved documents.

Summary Table: External Knowledge Sources

Method	Description	Example Use Cases
Retrieval-Augmented Generation (RAG)	Combines retrieval of relevant documents with text generation.	Open-domain question answering, summarization.
Knowledge Graph Integration	Merges structured entity data with text embeddings.	Medical diagnosis, legal document analysis.
Memory Networks	Uses external memory for storing and retrieving facts.	Conversational agents, dynamic information retrieval.
Prompt Engineering	Designs prompts that incorporate external facts or context.	Chatbots, real-time information systems.

8.4 Transfer Learning and Domain Adaptation Strategies

Transfer learning and domain adaptation are pivotal strategies in leveraging pre-trained models for specialized applications. These approaches allow a model trained on a broad dataset to be adapted efficiently to a specific domain or task, thereby saving time, computational resources, and often improving performance.

Transfer Learning Overview

Transfer Learning involves using a model pre-trained on a large, generic dataset as the starting point for fine-tuning on a specific task. The intuition behind transfer learning is that the pre-trained model has already learned useful features and patterns from its vast training data, which can be beneficial when adapting to a new task with limited data.

- **Key Benefits:**
  - **Reduced Training Time:** Fine-tuning a pre-trained model requires far less data and time compared to training from scratch.
  - **Better Generalization:** Leveraging learned representations often results in better performance, especially in low-data regimes.
  - **Cost Efficiency:** Utilizing existing models reduces the computational expense associated with large-scale training.

Domain Adaptation Strategies

Domain Adaptation focuses on modifying a model so that it performs well in a specific domain different from its original training data. This is particularly important when the target domain has different vocabulary, style, or contextual nuances.

Strategies for Domain Adaptation:

1. **Intermediate Fine-Tuning:**
   Before fine-tuning on the final task, the model is first fine-tuned on a domain-specific dataset. This intermediate step helps bridge the gap between the general pre-trained model and the specialized domain.
2. **Multi-Domain Training:**
   Simultaneously fine-tuning the model on data from multiple domains can help it learn domain-invariant features while still capturing domain-specific variations.
3. **Domain-Adversarial Training:**
   Incorporate adversarial objectives that encourage the model to learn

representations that are invariant to domain differences. This helps in reducing domain-specific biases.

4. **Selective Freezing:**
   Freezing certain layers (usually the early layers that capture general language features) while fine-tuning others can help maintain a balance between preserving general knowledge and learning domain-specific nuances.

Example: Intermediate Fine-Tuning

The following example demonstrates intermediate fine-tuning using the Hugging Face Transformers library. In this scenario, a pre-trained model is first fine-tuned on a generic domain-specific dataset (e.g., scientific articles) before being further fine-tuned on a more specialized task (e.g., biomedical question answering).

python

```python
from transformers import AutoTokenizer, AutoModelForQuestionAnswering, Trainer, TrainingArguments

from datasets import load_dataset


# Step 1: Intermediate Fine-Tuning on a Domain-Specific Dataset

intermediate_model_name = "bert-base-uncased"

tokenizer = AutoTokenizer.from_pretrained(intermediate_model_name)

model = AutoModelForQuestionAnswering.from_pretrained(intermediate_model_name)


# Load a domain-specific dataset (e.g., a scientific QA dataset)

intermediate_dataset = load_dataset("squad")  # Example; replace with a domain-specific dataset


# Tokenize the intermediate dataset
```

153

```python
def tokenize_qa(examples):

    return tokenizer(examples["question"], examples["context"],
truncation=True, padding="max_length", max_length=384)


tokenized_intermediate = intermediate_dataset.map(tokenize_qa,
batched=True)


# Define training arguments for intermediate fine-tuning
training_args_intermediate = TrainingArguments(

    output_dir="./intermediate_finetuned_model",

    num_train_epochs=2,

    per_device_train_batch_size=8,

    learning_rate=3e-5,

    evaluation_strategy="epoch",
)


# Initialize the Trainer for intermediate fine-tuning
trainer_intermediate = Trainer(

    model=model,

    args=training_args_intermediate,

    train_dataset=tokenized_intermediate["train"],

    eval_dataset=tokenized_intermediate["validation"],
)
```

```python
# Fine-tune the model on the intermediate dataset

trainer_intermediate.train()


# Step 2: Further Fine-Tuning on the Specialized Task
# Assume you have a specialized biomedical QA dataset loaded similarly

biomedical_dataset = load_dataset("biomedical_qa_dataset")  # Hypothetical dataset

tokenized_biomedical = biomedical_dataset.map(tokenize_qa, batched=True)


training_args_biomedical = TrainingArguments(
    output_dir="./biomedical_finetuned_model",
    num_train_epochs=3,
    per_device_train_batch_size=8,
    learning_rate=2e-5,
    evaluation_strategy="epoch",
)


trainer_biomedical = Trainer(
    model=model,
    args=training_args_biomedical,
    train_dataset=tokenized_biomedical["train"],
    eval_dataset=tokenized_biomedical["validation"],
)
```

```
# Fine-tune the model on the biomedical dataset

trainer_biomedical.train()
```

Explanation:

- **Intermediate Fine-Tuning:**
  The model is first fine-tuned on a generic QA dataset (e.g., SQuAD) to adjust its representations towards question-answering tasks in a scientific context.
- **Specialized Fine-Tuning:**
  The same model is then further fine-tuned on a specialized dataset (e.g., biomedical QA). This sequential adaptation helps the model learn both general QA patterns and domain-specific nuances.

Summary Table: Transfer Learning and Domain Adaptation Strategies

Strategy	Description	Benefits
Transfer Learning	Fine-tuning a pre-trained model on a new, task-specific dataset.	Reduced training time, improved generalization.
Intermediate Fine-Tuning	An additional fine-tuning step on a domain-specific dataset before the final task.	Bridges the gap between general and specialized domains.
Multi-Domain Training	Fine-tuning on data from multiple domains simultaneously.	Learns domain-invariant features while capturing nuances.

Domain-Adversarial Training	Incorporates adversarial objectives to minimize domain-specific biases.	Reduces domain bias, improves cross-domain performance.
Selective Freezing	Freezes early layers to preserve general knowledge while fine-tuning later layers for domain-specific tasks.	Balances preservation of pre-trained features and new learning.

Incorporating external knowledge sources and leveraging transfer learning with robust domain adaptation strategies are crucial for advancing the performance and versatility of large language models. By integrating methods such as retrieval-augmented generation, knowledge graph incorporation, and memory networks, models gain access to rich, supplementary information that enhances contextual understanding. Meanwhile, strategies like intermediate fine-tuning, multi-domain training, and selective freezing enable a model to efficiently transfer its broad, pre-trained knowledge to specialized tasks and domains.

The detailed explanations, code examples, and summary tables provided in this chapter equip you with advanced techniques to further fine-tune and optimize language models for complex, real-world applications. These strategies not only enhance performance but also promote adaptability and robustness across a wide range of scenarios.

Chapter 9: Parameter-Efficient Fine-Tuning Methods

As large language models (LLMs) continue to grow in size and complexity, fine-tuning them for specific tasks using full-parameter updates can be computationally expensive and resource intensive. Parameter-efficient fine-tuning methods offer an attractive alternative by modifying only a small subset of the model's parameters or by adding lightweight modules. This chapter focuses on two popular approaches: Low-Rank Adaptation (LoRA) and adapter modules combined with prompt tuning. Both methods aim to achieve competitive performance with significantly reduced training costs.

9.1 Introduction to Low-Rank Adaptation (LoRA)

Overview

Low-Rank Adaptation (LoRA) is a technique that adapts large pre-trained models by injecting trainable low-rank matrices into the network's weight matrices while keeping the original weights frozen. This approach drastically reduces the number of parameters that need to be updated during fine-tuning, making the process more efficient and less prone to overfitting, particularly when dealing with limited task-specific data.

How LoRA Works

- **Weight Decomposition:**
  LoRA assumes that the update needed for a weight matrix WW can be approximated by a low-rank matrix decomposition. Instead of updating WW directly, it introduces two trainable matrices, AA and BB, where:
  $$\Delta W \approx BA \Delta W \approx BA$$
  Here, $A \in R^{r \times d} A \in R^{r \times d}$ and $B \in R^{d \times r} B \in R^{d \times r}$ with $r \ll d r \ll d$, meaning that only a small number of parameters are learned.
- **Frozen Base Model:**
  The pre-trained model's weights remain unchanged. Only the low-rank matrices AA and BB are updated during fine-tuning. This not only reduces memory usage but also makes the process faster.
- **Integration into Existing Architectures:**
  LoRA can be applied to various layers, such as the attention modules in transformer architectures, without altering the original model structure.

Benefits of LoRA

- **Parameter Efficiency:**
  By updating only a few additional parameters, LoRA reduces computational overhead and storage requirements.
- **Faster Convergence:**
  Since the majority of the model remains unchanged, the training process converges faster on task-specific data.
- **Flexibility:**
  LoRA can be integrated with different model architectures and tasks with minimal modifications.

Code Example: Fine-Tuning with LoRA Using PEFT

Below is an example using the Hugging Face PEFT (Parameter-Efficient Fine-Tuning) library, which supports LoRA. In this example, we fine-tune a pre-trained BERT model for a classification task using LoRA.

python

```python
# Install the peft package if not already installed:

# !pip install peft


import torch

from transformers import AutoModelForSequenceClassification, AutoTokenizer, TrainingArguments, Trainer

from peft import get_peft_model, LoraConfig, TaskType

from datasets import load_dataset


# Load a pre-trained model and tokenizer

model_name = "bert-base-uncased"
```

```python
model =
AutoModelForSequenceClassification.from_pretrained(model_name,
num_labels=2)

tokenizer = AutoTokenizer.from_pretrained(model_name)


# Define a LoRA configuration

lora_config = LoraConfig(

    task_type=TaskType.SEQ_CLS,

    inference_mode=False,

    r=8,        # Low-rank dimension

    lora_alpha=32, # Scaling factor

    lora_dropout=0.1

)


# Wrap the model with LoRA

model = get_peft_model(model, lora_config)

model.print_trainable_parameters()


# Load a dataset (using the IMDB dataset for sentiment analysis as an
example)

dataset = load_dataset("imdb")

train_dataset = dataset["train"].shuffle(seed=42).select(range(2000))

test_dataset = dataset["test"].shuffle(seed=42).select(range(500))


# Tokenize the dataset
```

```python
def tokenize_function(examples):

    return tokenizer(examples["text"], padding="max_length",
truncation=True, max_length=128)


train_dataset = train_dataset.map(tokenize_function, batched=True)

test_dataset = test_dataset.map(tokenize_function, batched=True)


# Define training arguments
training_args = TrainingArguments(
    output_dir="./lora_finetuned_bert",
    evaluation_strategy="epoch",
    learning_rate=2e-5,
    per_device_train_batch_size=16,
    per_device_eval_batch_size=16,
    num_train_epochs=3,
    weight_decay=0.01,
)


# Initialize Trainer with the LoRA-wrapped model
trainer = Trainer(
    model=model,
    args=training_args,
    train_dataset=train_dataset,
    eval_dataset=test_dataset,
```

```
)
```

```
# Fine-tune the model
```

```
trainer.train()
```

Explanation:

- **PEFT Integration:**
  The get_peft_model function wraps the pre-trained model with the LoRA configuration, injecting low-rank matrices into appropriate layers.
- **LoRA Configuration:**
  Parameters such as the rank rr, scaling factor lora_alphalora_alpha, and dropout are defined.
- **Training:**
  The Trainer API from Hugging Face is used to fine-tune the model on the IMDB dataset, updating only the LoRA parameters.

Summary Table: LoRA

Aspect	Description
Core Idea	Approximate weight updates with low-rank matrices (BA) instead of updating full weights.
Parameter Efficiency	Only additional matrices AA and BB are trainable, significantly reducing the number of updated parameters.

Benefits	Faster convergence, lower memory usage, and easier adaptation to new tasks.

9.2 Adapter Modules and Prompt Tuning

Overview

Adapter modules and prompt tuning are alternative parameter-efficient methods that allow models to be fine-tuned with minimal changes to the base model. Both methods involve adding small, trainable components that interface with the frozen pre-trained model.

Adapter Modules

What Are Adapter Modules?

Adapter modules are lightweight neural network layers inserted between the layers of a pre-trained model. During fine-tuning, only the adapter parameters are updated while the original model weights remain frozen. This approach is particularly useful when adapting models to multiple tasks or domains without retraining the entire network.

How Adapter Modules Work:

- **Insertion Points:**
  Adapter modules are typically added between the transformer layers or after the feed-forward networks.
- **Architecture:**
  An adapter module often consists of a down-projection (reducing dimensionality), a non-linear activation (e.g., ReLU), and an up-projection (restoring dimensionality).
- **Residual Connection:**
  The output of the adapter is usually added back to the original layer's output, forming a residual connection.

Benefits of Adapter Modules:

- **Modularity:**
  Different adapters can be used for different tasks, allowing a single model to be quickly adapted to multiple domains.
- **Parameter Efficiency:**
  Only a small fraction of parameters are updated, reducing computational overhead and storage requirements.
- **Flexibility:**
  Adapters can be applied to various architectures and tasks without significant modifications.

Code Example: Using Adapter Modules with PEFT

Below is an example that demonstrates how to add adapters to a pre-trained model using the PEFT library for a classification task.

python

```python
from peft import get_peft_model, AdapterConfig, TaskType


# Define an adapter configuration
adapter_config = AdapterConfig(
    task_type=TaskType.SEQ_CLS,
    adapter_dim=64,    # Dimensionality of the adapter bottleneck
    non_linearity="relu",
    dropout=0.1
)


# Wrap the model with adapters
model = get_peft_model(model, adapter_config)
model.print_trainable_parameters()
```

```
# The remaining training pipeline is similar to the LoRA example.
```

Explanation:

- **Adapter Configuration:**
  The AdapterConfig specifies the adapter bottleneck dimension, activation
  function, and dropout rate.
- **Model Wrapping:**
  The get_peft_model function is reused to wrap the pre-trained model with
  adapter modules. Only the adapter parameters will be updated during fine-
  tuning.

Prompt Tuning

What is Prompt Tuning?

Prompt tuning involves learning a set of continuous prompt vectors that are prepended
to the input text. Instead of modifying the model weights, only these prompt vectors are
optimized during fine-tuning. This approach is especially useful for models that are
deployed as black boxes or in scenarios where storage or update constraints exist.

How Prompt Tuning Works:

- **Continuous Prompts:**
  A small set of trainable embeddings (prompts) is concatenated with the input
  embeddings.
- **Frozen Base Model:**
  The pre-trained model remains frozen, and only the prompt embeddings are
  updated.
- **Task-Specific Guidance:**
  The learned prompts steer the model's behavior toward the desired output
  without extensive modifications to the model.

Benefits of Prompt Tuning:

- **Minimal Parameter Updates:**
  Only the prompt embeddings are trained, resulting in extremely low
  computational overhead.

- **Ease of Deployment:**
  Prompt-tuned models can be deployed without altering the base model, making them suitable for environments with strict update constraints.
- **Versatility:**
  Multiple prompts can be learned for different tasks or domains, allowing rapid adaptation.

Summary Table: Adapter Modules vs. Prompt Tuning

Method	Mechanism	Benefits	Use Cases
Adapter Modules	Inserting lightweight, trainable layers between existing layers.	Modular, efficient multi-task adaptation, retains original model structure.	Multi-domain fine-tuning, resource-constrained environments.
Prompt Tuning	Learning a set of continuous prompt embeddings added to the input.	Minimal parameter updates, easy deployment, model remains entirely frozen.	Scenarios with strict update constraints, rapid prototyping.

Parameter-efficient fine-tuning methods such as LoRA, adapter modules, and prompt tuning provide powerful alternatives to full-parameter updates. LoRA achieves efficiency by approximating weight updates using low-rank matrices, while adapter modules introduce additional lightweight layers that can be tailored for multiple tasks. Prompt tuning, on the other hand, optimizes only a small set of prompt embeddings, guiding the model's behavior without modifying the base model. These techniques not only reduce computational and storage requirements but also facilitate rapid adaptation and deployment of large language models across diverse tasks and domains.

With the detailed explanations, comprehensive code examples, and comparative tables provided in this chapter, you now have a solid foundation for applying parameter-efficient fine-tuning methods to your projects. These strategies enable you to harness the full power of large language models while optimizing resources and ensuring flexibility in real-world applications.

9.3 Comparison of Parameter-Efficient Methods

Parameter-efficient fine-tuning methods aim to adapt large pre-trained models to new tasks with minimal changes to the overall parameter count. The primary methods include Low-Rank Adaptation (LoRA), adapter modules, and prompt tuning. Each approach offers distinct advantages and trade-offs, making them suitable for different scenarios. In this section, we compare these methods in terms of their mechanisms, efficiency, flexibility, and typical use cases.

Key Methods Overview

- **Low-Rank Adaptation (LoRA):**
  LoRA introduces two small trainable matrices into certain weight matrices of the pre-trained model. By approximating the weight update as a low-rank factorization (i.e., $\Delta W \approx BA \Delta W \approx BA$), only the additional matrices AA and BB are trained, while the base model remains frozen.
- **Adapter Modules:**
  Adapter modules are lightweight neural network layers inserted between existing layers of the model. They typically consist of a down-projection, a non-linear activation (e.g., ReLU), and an up-projection. During fine-tuning, only these adapter parameters are updated, leaving the pre-trained weights unchanged.
- **Prompt Tuning:**
  Prompt tuning involves learning a small set of continuous prompt vectors that are prepended to the input text. The pre-trained model remains entirely frozen, and only the prompt embeddings are optimized. These learned prompts guide the model's output for a specific task.

Comparative Analysis

Below is a detailed comparison table summarizing the key characteristics of these methods:

Aspect	Low-Rank Adaptation (LoRA)	Adapter Modules	Prompt Tuning

Mechanism	Injects trainable low-rank matrices (AA and BB) into selected weight matrices.	Inserts small, additional neural network layers between pre-trained layers.	Learns task-specific continuous prompt embeddings added to the input.
Parameter Update Scope	Only the low-rank matrices are updated; the base model is frozen.	Only the adapter parameters are updated; the base model remains frozen.	Only the prompt embeddings are optimized; no model weights are modified.
Computational Overhead	Very low; requires storage and computation for two small matrices per adapted layer.	Low to moderate; depends on the adapter size and number of inserted modules.	Extremely low; only a handful of prompt vectors are optimized.
Flexibility	Can be applied to various layers (e.g., attention modules) in transformer models.	Highly modular; adapters can be easily added or removed and swapped for different tasks.	Ideal when the base model must remain unchanged, such as in black-box settings.
Training Efficiency	Fast convergence due to minimal parameter updates and	Efficient in multi-task or multi-domain settings as adapters can be	Extremely efficient in terms of both time and memory footprint.

	preserved pre-trained weights.	shared or specialized.	
Typical Use Cases	Fine-tuning for tasks with limited data where preserving the pre-trained model is crucial.	Multi-domain or multi-task learning, where separate adapters can be learned for each scenario.	Scenarios with strict resource constraints or where model updates are not feasible (e.g., cloud APIs).

Code Example Comparison

Below are brief code excerpts illustrating how each method is typically implemented using the Hugging Face ecosystem and its associated libraries (e.g., PEFT):

LoRA Example:

python

```python
from peft import get_peft_model, LoraConfig, TaskType

from transformers import AutoModelForSequenceClassification


model_name = "bert-base-uncased"
model = AutoModelForSequenceClassification.from_pretrained(model_name, num_labels=2)


lora_config = LoraConfig(
    task_type=TaskType.SEQ_CLS,
```

```python
    r=8,

    lora_alpha=32,

    lora_dropout=0.1

)

model = get_peft_model(model, lora_config)

model.print_trainable_parameters()
```

Adapter Modules Example:

python

```python
from peft import get_peft_model, AdapterConfig, TaskType

from transformers import AutoModelForSequenceClassification


model_name = "bert-base-uncased"

model = AutoModelForSequenceClassification.from_pretrained(model_name, num_labels=2)


adapter_config = AdapterConfig(

    task_type=TaskType.SEQ_CLS,

    adapter_dim=64,

    non_linearity="relu",

    dropout=0.1

)
```

```python
model = get_peft_model(model, adapter_config)

model.print_trainable_parameters()
```

Prompt Tuning Example:

Prompt tuning implementations often use specialized libraries or configurations. An example of setting up prompt tuning with a hypothetical library might look like:

python

```python
from transformers import AutoModelForSequenceClassification, AutoTokenizer


model_name = "bert-base-uncased"

model = AutoModelForSequenceClassification.from_pretrained(model_name, num_labels=2)

tokenizer = AutoTokenizer.from_pretrained(model_name)


# Assume we have a function to add continuous prompt embeddings.

# This is a simplified illustration.

def add_prompt_tuning(model, prompt_length=5):

    # Create prompt embeddings as trainable parameters

    prompt_embeddings = torch.nn.Parameter(torch.randn(prompt_length, model.config.hidden_size))

    model.prompt_embeddings = prompt_embeddings

    return model
```

```
model = add_prompt_tuning(model, prompt_length=5)

print("Prompt tuning applied. Only prompt embeddings will be updated.")
```

Explanation:
Each code snippet illustrates how minimal changes to the base model are sufficient to achieve task-specific fine-tuning through different mechanisms.

9.4 Use Cases and Practical Applications

Parameter-efficient fine-tuning methods are particularly valuable in real-world scenarios where computational resources, storage, or update frequency are limited. This section outlines various use cases and practical applications where these techniques have a significant impact.

Use Cases

1. **Multi-Domain Deployments:**
   - **Scenario:** A single model is required to serve multiple domains, such as customer support, legal document analysis, and medical advice.
   - **Solution:** Adapter modules allow different adapters to be applied for each domain while using a shared base model. This modularity facilitates switching between tasks without retraining the entire model.
2. **Resource-Constrained Environments:**
   - **Scenario:** Deployment on edge devices or mobile applications where computational power and memory are limited.
   - **Solution:** Prompt tuning and LoRA offer extremely lightweight adaptations that require minimal additional storage and computation, making them ideal for such environments.
3. **Rapid Prototyping and Experimentation:**
   - **Scenario:** When testing multiple hypotheses or iterating quickly over different tasks, it is inefficient to fine-tune the entire model repeatedly.
   - **Solution:** Parameter-efficient methods allow rapid experimentation by updating only a small fraction of the model, significantly reducing training time and computational cost.
4. **Cloud-Based API Models:**

- ○ **Scenario:** Large language models are deployed as APIs in the cloud, where updating the entire model might not be feasible due to deployment constraints or stability concerns.
- ○ **Solution:** Prompt tuning is particularly attractive here because it leaves the core model intact while only modifying the input prompts. This approach maintains consistency and reliability while enabling customization.

5. **Limited Data Regimes:**
   - ○ **Scenario:** In domains where labeled data is scarce, full model fine-tuning can lead to overfitting.
   - ○ **Solution:** Methods like LoRA and adapter modules reduce the risk of overfitting by limiting the number of trainable parameters, enabling effective fine-tuning even with small datasets.

Practical Applications

- **Sentiment Analysis in Niche Markets:**
  A company specializing in a specific industry (e.g., finance) can use adapter modules to fine-tune a sentiment analysis model for its unique vocabulary and sentiment expressions without compromising the general language understanding.
- **Legal Document Classification:**
  Law firms can employ LoRA to fine-tune pre-trained models on vast legal corpora. The low-rank adaptation allows the model to capture the intricacies of legal language efficiently while minimizing the computational cost.
- **Personalized Chatbots:**
  By using prompt tuning, developers can quickly adapt a general conversational model to reflect individual user preferences or specific customer service scenarios. This approach is beneficial for applications requiring frequent updates based on user feedback.
- **Healthcare Diagnostics:**
  Multi-domain fine-tuning enables the development of models that can handle both general medical inquiries and specialized diagnostics for particular conditions. Adapter modules can be applied to switch between different medical sub-domains seamlessly.

Example: Multi-Domain Application with Adapters

Consider an application where a single model needs to operate in both legal and medical domains. Using adapter modules, different sets of adapter parameters can be trained for each domain. During deployment, the system selects the appropriate adapter based on the context of the input.

python

```python
# Pseudocode illustration for a multi-domain adapter setup


# Load the base model

model = AutoModelForSequenceClassification.from_pretrained("bert-base-uncased", num_labels=2)


# Configure and add adapter for legal domain

legal_adapter_config = AdapterConfig(task_type=TaskType.SEQ_CLS, adapter_dim=64, non_linearity="relu", dropout=0.1)

model = add_adapter(model, "legal", legal_adapter_config)


# Configure and add adapter for medical domain

medical_adapter_config = AdapterConfig(task_type=TaskType.SEQ_CLS, adapter_dim=64, non_linearity="relu", dropout=0.1)

model = add_adapter(model, "medical", medical_adapter_config)


# To switch domains during inference:

current_domain = "legal"  # or "medical"

model.set_active_adapters(current_domain)


# Now, use the model as usual for prediction

inputs = tokenizer("Your legal document text here", return_tensors="pt")

outputs = model(**inputs)
```

```
predictions = outputs.logits.argmax(dim=-1)

print("Predictions:", predictions)
```

Explanation:

- **Adapter Addition:**
  Separate adapters for legal and medical domains are added to the base model.
- **Domain Switching:**
  During inference, the appropriate adapter is activated based on the input's context.
- **Efficiency:**
  This modular approach allows a single model to adapt dynamically without full re-training.

Summary Table: Use Cases and Applications

Use Case	Method	Benefits
Multi-Domain Deployments	Adapter Modules	Modular adaptation for different domains; shared base model reduces overall maintenance costs.
Resource-Constrained Environments	Prompt Tuning, LoRA	Minimal parameter updates; ideal for devices with limited computational and memory resources.
Rapid Prototyping and Experimentation	All methods (LoRA, Adapters, Prompt Tuning)	Fast training iterations with reduced computational overhead; flexibility to test multiple hypotheses.

Cloud-Based API Models	Prompt Tuning	Base model remains unchanged; updates are lightweight and do not disrupt existing deployment.
Limited Data Regimes	LoRA, Adapter Modules	Reduced risk of overfitting; efficient fine-tuning with a small number of trainable parameters.

Parameter-efficient fine-tuning methods provide a scalable and resource-friendly approach to adapting large language models for specialized tasks and domains. By comparing methods like LoRA, adapter modules, and prompt tuning, we see that each offers unique benefits—from minimal computational overhead to the ability to seamlessly switch between multiple domains. Real-world applications, ranging from sentiment analysis in niche markets to multi-domain chatbots and healthcare diagnostics, highlight the practical value of these techniques.

With comprehensive comparisons, detailed code examples, and clear use case illustrations, this section equips you with the knowledge to choose and implement the right parameter-efficient strategy for your specific needs. Whether your goal is rapid prototyping, efficient deployment in resource-limited settings, or robust multi-domain performance, these methods enable you to harness the full power of large language models while optimizing for efficiency and flexibility.

Chapter 10: Hyperparameter Optimization and Training Strategies

Optimizing hyperparameters is a critical aspect of fine-tuning large language models (LLMs). The right set of hyperparameters can significantly improve convergence, generalization, and overall model performance. In this chapter, we explore best practices for hyperparameter tuning and discuss various search methods such as grid search, random search, and Bayesian optimization.

10.1 Best Practices for Hyperparameter Tuning

Hyperparameter tuning is the process of systematically searching for the best combination of hyperparameters—such as learning rate, batch size, number of training epochs, and dropout rate—that yield optimal model performance. Here are some best practices to follow:

1. Define Your Objective Clearly

- **Evaluation Metrics:**
  Determine which metric(s) best reflect your model's performance (e.g., accuracy, F1-score, BLEU score). Use these metrics consistently to compare different hyperparameter configurations.
- **Validation Strategy:**
  Use a dedicated validation set or cross-validation to reliably assess model performance during tuning. This prevents overfitting to the training set.

2. Start with a Coarse Search

- **Broad Ranges:**
  Begin with a wide range of values for each hyperparameter. This helps you understand the general sensitivity of the model to different hyperparameter settings.
- **Limited Combinations:**
  Evaluate a limited number of combinations initially to narrow down promising regions in the hyperparameter space.

3. Fine-Tune Based on Initial Findings

- **Refined Ranges:**
  Once promising hyperparameter ranges are identified, narrow the search range and focus on fine-tuning around those values.
- **Incremental Adjustments:**
  Use smaller step sizes or higher resolution in promising regions.

4. Use Learning Rate Warmup and Decay

- **Warmup:**
  Gradually increase the learning rate at the beginning of training to help stabilize convergence.
- **Decay:**
  Decrease the learning rate as training progresses to allow the model to settle into a local minimum. Popular decay schedules include step decay, exponential decay, and cosine annealing.

5. Monitor and Record Experiments

- **Experiment Tracking:**
  Use experiment tracking tools (e.g., MLflow, Weights & Biases) to log hyperparameter settings, training loss, validation metrics, and other details for each run.
- **Reproducibility:**
  Save configurations and random seeds to ensure that experiments can be reproduced.

6. Consider Resource Constraints

- **Batch Size and Memory:**
  Choose batch sizes that balance computational efficiency with available GPU/CPU memory.
- **Training Time:**
  Use early stopping or a limited number of epochs during initial experiments to save time.

Example: Hyperparameter Tuning Best Practices in Code

Below is a simple example using Python that demonstrates setting up a training loop with logging for hyperparameter tuning. In this case, we use a learning rate warmup strategy with a cosine annealing scheduler.

python

```python
import torch

import torch.nn as nn

import torch.optim as optim

from torch.optim.lr_scheduler import CosineAnnealingLR

from transformers import AutoModelForSequenceClassification,
AutoTokenizer

from transformers import TrainingArguments, Trainer

from datasets import load_dataset


# Load model and tokenizer (example: fine-tuning BERT on a classification
task)

model_name = "bert-base-uncased"

model =
AutoModelForSequenceClassification.from_pretrained(model_name,
num_labels=2)

tokenizer = AutoTokenizer.from_pretrained(model_name)


# Load dataset (using IMDB for sentiment analysis as an example)

dataset = load_dataset("imdb")

train_dataset = dataset["train"].shuffle(seed=42).select(range(2000))

val_dataset = dataset["test"].shuffle(seed=42).select(range(500))


# Define a tokenization function

def tokenize_function(examples):
```

```python
    return tokenizer(examples["text"], padding="max_length",
truncation=True, max_length=128)


train_dataset = train_dataset.map(tokenize_function, batched=True)

val_dataset = val_dataset.map(tokenize_function, batched=True)


# Define training arguments
training_args = TrainingArguments(
    output_dir="./results",
    num_train_epochs=3,
    per_device_train_batch_size=16,
    per_device_eval_batch_size=16,
    learning_rate=2e-5,
    weight_decay=0.01,
    evaluation_strategy="epoch",
    logging_steps=50,
    save_total_limit=2,
)


# Create a Trainer instance
trainer = Trainer(
    model=model,
    args=training_args,
    train_dataset=train_dataset,
```

```python
    eval_dataset=val_dataset,
)
```

To integrate a learning rate scheduler, one would typically override the optimizer and scheduler:

```python
optimizer = optim.AdamW(model.parameters(), lr=2e-5, weight_decay=0.01)

scheduler = CosineAnnealingLR(optimizer, T_max=len(train_dataset)//16, eta_min=1e-6)
```

```python
# A training loop could log metrics and adjust hyperparameters accordingly
for epoch in range(3):
    model.train()
    for batch in trainer.get_train_dataloader():
        optimizer.zero_grad()
        outputs = model(input_ids=batch["input_ids"],
            attention_mask=batch["attention_mask"],
            labels=batch["labels"])
        loss = outputs.loss
        loss.backward()
        optimizer.step()
        scheduler.step()
    print(f"Epoch {epoch+1} completed.")
```

Explanation:

- **Warmup and Scheduler:**
  The code uses the cosine annealing scheduler to adjust the learning rate dynamically during training.
- **Experiment Logging:**
  The logging_steps parameter helps track progress, and saving limits ensure that only the best model checkpoints are kept.
- **Validation Strategy:**
  A separate validation dataset is used to evaluate performance after each epoch.

10.2 Grid Search, Random Search, and Bayesian Optimization

Different search methods can be employed to explore the hyperparameter space. The three most common methods are grid search, random search, and Bayesian optimization.

Grid Search

Grid Search involves defining a set of discrete values for each hyperparameter and exhaustively evaluating every possible combination. This method is simple and guarantees that all specified combinations are tried, but it can be computationally expensive when the hyperparameter space is large.

Pros:

- Easy to implement.
- Guarantees coverage of all specified combinations.

Cons:

- Inefficient for high-dimensional spaces.
- May waste resources on unpromising combinations.

Example: Grid Search Pseudocode

python

```
learning_rates = [1e-5, 2e-5, 3e-5]

batch_sizes = [16, 32]
```

```python
epochs = [3, 4]

for lr in learning_rates:
  for batch_size in batch_sizes:
    for epoch in epochs:
      # Set up training arguments for each combination
      training_args = TrainingArguments(
        output_dir=f"./results_lr{lr}_bs{batch_size}_ep{epoch}",
        num_train_epochs=epoch,
        per_device_train_batch_size=batch_size,
        learning_rate=lr,
        evaluation_strategy="epoch",
      )
      # Initialize and train the model (using Trainer API)
      trainer = Trainer(
        model=model,
        args=training_args,
        train_dataset=train_dataset,
        eval_dataset=val_dataset,
      )
      trainer.train()
      # Evaluate and log results
      eval_results = trainer.evaluate()
```

```
    print(f"LR: {lr}, Batch Size: {batch_size}, Epochs: {epoch}, Results:
{eval_results}")
```

Random Search

Random Search selects random combinations of hyperparameters from predefined distributions. Research has shown that random search can be more efficient than grid search, especially when some hyperparameters have a greater impact on performance than others.

Pros:

- More efficient than grid search in many cases.
- Can explore a broader range of values.

Cons:

- Results can be variable; randomness may miss some optimal regions.

Example: Random Search Pseudocode

python

```
import random


# Define hyperparameter distributions

learning_rate_distribution = [1e-5, 2e-5, 3e-5, 4e-5, 5e-5]

batch_size_distribution = [16, 32, 64]

epoch_distribution = [3, 4, 5]


for i in range(10):  # 10 random combinations

    lr = random.choice(learning_rate_distribution)

    batch_size = random.choice(batch_size_distribution)
```

```python
epoch = random.choice(epoch_distribution)

# Set up training arguments for the random combination

training_args = TrainingArguments(

    output_dir=f"./results_random_{i}",

    num_train_epochs=epoch,

    per_device_train_batch_size=batch_size,

    learning_rate=lr,

    evaluation_strategy="epoch",

)

trainer = Trainer(

    model=model,

    args=training_args,

    train_dataset=train_dataset,

    eval_dataset=val_dataset,

)

trainer.train()

eval_results = trainer.evaluate()

print(f"Iteration {i}: LR: {lr}, Batch Size: {batch_size}, Epochs: {epoch}, Results: {eval_results}")
```

Bayesian Optimization

Bayesian Optimization is a more sophisticated method that models the hyperparameter search space using a probabilistic surrogate function. This method uses past evaluation results to predict which hyperparameter settings are likely to yield better performance, thereby focusing the search on promising regions.

Pros:

- Efficient in high-dimensional spaces.
- Focuses on promising regions of the hyperparameter space.

Cons:

- More complex to implement.
- May require integration with specialized libraries (e.g., Optuna, Hyperopt).

Example: Bayesian Optimization with Optuna

Below is an example of using the Optuna library to optimize hyperparameters for a model fine-tuning task.

python

```python
import optuna

from optuna.integration import PyTorchLightningPruningCallback

from transformers import TrainingArguments, Trainer


def objective(trial):
    # Suggest hyperparameters
    lr = trial.suggest_loguniform("learning_rate", 1e-5, 5e-5)

    batch_size = trial.suggest_categorical("batch_size", [16, 32, 64])

    epochs = trial.suggest_int("epochs", 3, 5)


    training_args = TrainingArguments(
        output_dir="./optuna_results",

        num_train_epochs=epochs,

        per_device_train_batch_size=batch_size,
```

```python
        learning_rate=lr,

        evaluation_strategy="epoch",

        logging_steps=50,

    )


    trainer = Trainer(

        model=model,

        args=training_args,

        train_dataset=train_dataset,

        eval_dataset=val_dataset,

    )


    # Train the model

    trainer.train()

    eval_results = trainer.evaluate()

    # Objective to minimize: validation loss or maximize accuracy

    return eval_results["eval_loss"]


# Create an Optuna study and optimize

study = optuna.create_study(direction="minimize")

study.optimize(objective, n_trials=10)


print("Best hyperparameters found:")
```

```
print(study.best_params)
```

Explanation:

- **Objective Function:**
  The function defines the hyperparameters to be tuned and returns a metric (e.g., validation loss) that the optimization process will minimize.
- **Optuna Study:**
  An Optuna study is created and run for a specified number of trials, and the best parameters are then printed.
- **Integration:**
  The example uses the Trainer API to integrate with the hyperparameter optimization process seamlessly.

Summary Table: Hyperparameter Search Methods

Method	Approach	Pros	Cons
Grid Search	Exhaustively evaluates all combinations	Simple; complete coverage of specified grid	Computationally expensive; inefficient for high-dimensional spaces
Random Search	Samples random combinations from distributions	More efficient; explores a broader range of values	May miss optimal regions due to randomness
Bayesian Optimization	Models the search space using a surrogate function	Efficient; focuses on promising regions	More complex; requires specialized libraries

Hyperparameter optimization is essential for fine-tuning large language models effectively. Following best practices—such as clearly defining objectives, starting with a coarse search, using learning rate warmup and decay, and monitoring experiments—ensures a systematic approach to tuning. Additionally, methods like grid search, random search, and Bayesian optimization each offer different advantages depending on the complexity of the hyperparameter space and available resources.

With detailed code examples, practical pseudocode, and summary tables provided in this chapter, you now have a solid understanding of how to approach hyperparameter optimization and implement training strategies that maximize model performance while managing computational efficiency.

10.3 Early Stopping, Checkpointing, and Resource Management

In deep learning, training large language models (LLMs) can be time-consuming and computationally expensive. To manage these challenges, several strategies help ensure efficient training and prevent wasted resources. In this section, we cover three important techniques: early stopping, checkpointing, and resource management.

Early Stopping

What Is Early Stopping?
Early stopping is a technique used to halt training when a monitored performance metric (e.g., validation loss) stops improving. By stopping training early, you prevent overfitting, save computational resources, and reduce training time.

Key Aspects:

- **Monitoring Metrics:**
  Typically, validation loss or accuracy is monitored. If these metrics do not improve after a certain number of epochs (called the "patience"), training is stopped.
- **Patience Parameter:**
  This parameter defines the number of epochs to wait before stopping once performance stops improving.
- **Improvement Threshold:**
  Sometimes a minimum improvement threshold is also set to account for minor fluctuations.

Example: Early Stopping in PyTorch with Hugging Face Trainer

python

```python
from transformers import TrainingArguments, Trainer, EarlyStoppingCallback

training_args = TrainingArguments(
    output_dir="./results",
    num_train_epochs=10,
    per_device_train_batch_size=16,
    per_device_eval_batch_size=16,
    evaluation_strategy="epoch",
    save_strategy="epoch",
    learning_rate=2e-5,
)

# Initialize EarlyStoppingCallback with a patience of 2 epochs
early_stopping = EarlyStoppingCallback(early_stopping_patience=2)

trainer = Trainer(
    model=model,
    args=training_args,
    train_dataset=train_dataset,
    eval_dataset=val_dataset,
    callbacks=[early_stopping],
```

```
)
```

trainer.train()

Explanation:

- **TrainingArguments:**
  Define key training parameters such as batch sizes, number of epochs, evaluation strategy, and learning rate.
- **EarlyStoppingCallback:**
  Integrated into the Trainer, it monitors the evaluation metric and stops training if no improvement is observed for 2 consecutive epochs.
- **Trainer:**
  The Trainer API orchestrates the training loop with early stopping functionality.

Checkpointing

What Is Checkpointing?
Checkpointing involves saving the model's state at regular intervals during training. This practice helps in recovering from interruptions and allows you to revert to a model state that performed well on the validation set.

Key Aspects:

- **Frequency:**
  Checkpoints can be saved after every epoch, a fixed number of training steps, or when an improvement is detected.
- **Storage Management:**
  It is important to manage storage by keeping only a limited number of checkpoints (using parameters such as save_total_limit) to prevent excessive disk usage.

Example: Checkpointing with Hugging Face Trainer

python

```python
training_args = TrainingArguments(

    output_dir="./checkpoint_dir",

    num_train_epochs=10,

    per_device_train_batch_size=16,

    per_device_eval_batch_size=16,

    evaluation_strategy="epoch",

    save_strategy="epoch",

    save_total_limit=3,  # Only keep the last 3 checkpoints

    learning_rate=2e-5,

)


trainer = Trainer(

    model=model,

    args=training_args,

    train_dataset=train_dataset,

    eval_dataset=val_dataset,

)


trainer.train()
```

Explanation:

- **Save Strategy:**
  The save_strategy="epoch" parameter instructs the Trainer to save a checkpoint after each epoch.

- **Save Total Limit:**
  The save_total_limit=3 parameter limits the number of saved checkpoints to the last three, ensuring that storage remains manageable.

Resource Management

What Is Resource Management?
Resource management involves strategies to efficiently utilize available computational resources (CPU, GPU, memory) during training.

Key Strategies:

- **Batch Size:**
  Choosing an appropriate batch size can balance GPU memory usage and training stability.
- **Mixed Precision Training:**
  Using mixed precision (FP16) reduces memory usage and speeds up training. Libraries like NVIDIA's Apex or native PyTorch AMP (Automatic Mixed Precision) support this.
- **Data Loading:**
  Efficient data loaders with multiple workers can prevent data loading bottlenecks.
- **Distributed Training:**
  For large-scale training, leveraging multiple GPUs or distributed systems can significantly reduce training time.

Example: Enabling Mixed Precision Training in Hugging Face Trainer

python

```python
training_args = TrainingArguments(

    output_dir="./results",

    num_train_epochs=10,

    per_device_train_batch_size=16,

    per_device_eval_batch_size=16,
```

```python
    evaluation_strategy="epoch",

    learning_rate=2e-5,

    fp16=True,  # Enable mixed precision training

)


trainer = Trainer(

    model=model,

    args=training_args,

    train_dataset=train_dataset,

    eval_dataset=val_dataset,

)


trainer.train()
```

Explanation:

- **Mixed Precision:**
  The fp16=True flag enables mixed precision training, reducing memory usage and potentially speeding up training.
- **Efficient Data Loading:**
  While not shown explicitly, using a DataLoader with an appropriate number of workers (via num_workers parameter) further enhances resource management.

10.4 Automated Tools and Frameworks

Automating hyperparameter tuning and training processes can greatly enhance productivity and ensure consistency across experiments. Various tools and frameworks have emerged to facilitate this automation.

Automated Hyperparameter Tuning Tools

1. **Optuna:**
   A flexible hyperparameter optimization framework that uses Bayesian optimization to find the best hyperparameters efficiently. Optuna integrates well with PyTorch and Hugging Face.
2. **Ray Tune:**
   A scalable hyperparameter tuning library that supports various search algorithms (grid search, random search, Bayesian optimization) and distributed training.
3. **Hyperopt:**
   Uses Bayesian optimization and has been widely used in machine learning research for hyperparameter tuning.

Example: Hyperparameter Optimization with Optuna

python

```python
import optuna

from optuna.integration import PyTorchLightningPruningCallback

from transformers import TrainingArguments, Trainer


def objective(trial):
    # Suggest hyperparameters
    lr = trial.suggest_loguniform("learning_rate", 1e-5, 5e-5)

    batch_size = trial.suggest_categorical("batch_size", [16, 32])

    epochs = trial.suggest_int("epochs", 3, 5)


    training_args = TrainingArguments(
        output_dir="./optuna_results",

        num_train_epochs=epochs,
```

```python
        per_device_train_batch_size=batch_size,
        per_device_eval_batch_size=batch_size,
        learning_rate=lr,
        evaluation_strategy="epoch",
        logging_steps=50,
    )

    trainer = Trainer(
        model=model,
        args=training_args,
        train_dataset=train_dataset,
        eval_dataset=val_dataset,
    )


    trainer.train()
    eval_results = trainer.evaluate()
    return eval_results["eval_loss"]


study = optuna.create_study(direction="minimize")
study.optimize(objective, n_trials=10)


print("Best hyperparameters:", study.best_params)
```

Explanation:

- **Objective Function:**
  Defines the hyperparameter search space and returns the evaluation loss.
- **Optuna Study:**
  Runs the optimization over 10 trials, selecting hyperparameters that minimize the evaluation loss.
- **Integration:**
  Optuna seamlessly integrates with the Trainer API for hyperparameter optimization.

Automated Training Frameworks

1. **Hugging Face Trainer API:**
   Provides a high-level interface to manage training loops, checkpointing, logging, and evaluation. It significantly reduces boilerplate code.
2. **MLflow:**
   An end-to-end platform for managing the machine learning lifecycle, including experiment tracking, model packaging, and deployment.
3. **Weights & Biases (W&B):**
   Offers experiment tracking, visualization, and collaboration tools to streamline the training and evaluation process.
4. **Ray Train:**
   Part of the Ray ecosystem, it enables distributed training and hyperparameter tuning, allowing you to scale experiments across multiple GPUs or nodes.

Example: Using Weights & Biases for Experiment Tracking

python

```python
# First, install Weights & Biases if not already installed:

# !pip install wandb


import wandb

from transformers import TrainingArguments, Trainer
```

```python
# Initialize Weights & Biases

wandb.init(project="llm-finetuning", entity="your-entity-name")


training_args = TrainingArguments(

    output_dir="./results",

    num_train_epochs=3,

    per_device_train_batch_size=16,

    per_device_eval_batch_size=16,

    learning_rate=2e-5,

    evaluation_strategy="epoch",

    logging_steps=50,

    report_to="wandb",  # Integrate with W&B

)


trainer = Trainer(

    model=model,

    args=training_args,

    train_dataset=train_dataset,

    eval_dataset=val_dataset,

)


trainer.train()
```

Explanation:

- **W&B Integration:**
  By setting report_to="wandb" in the TrainingArguments, training metrics are automatically logged to Weights & Biases.
- **Experiment Tracking:**
  This integration helps monitor training in real-time, compare experiments, and facilitate collaboration.

Summary Table: Automated Tools and Frameworks

Tool/Frame work	Purpose	Key Features
Optuna	Hyperparameter optimization	Bayesian optimization, flexible search space, integration with PyTorch
Ray Tune	Scalable hyperparameter tuning	Supports grid, random, and Bayesian search; distributed training support
Hugging Face Trainer	Simplifies training loop, checkpointing, and logging	High-level API; easy integration with Transformers models
MLflow	End-to-end ML lifecycle management	Experiment tracking, model packaging, and deployment

Weights & Biases	Experiment tracking and visualization	Real-time logging, collaboration, and detailed visualization

Efficient hyperparameter optimization and training strategies are essential for maximizing model performance while managing computational resources. Techniques such as early stopping, checkpointing, and effective resource management help prevent overfitting and reduce training time. Automated tools and frameworks like Optuna, Ray Tune, the Hugging Face Trainer API, MLflow, and Weights & Biases further streamline these processes by automating repetitive tasks and providing insightful experiment tracking.

By following best practices and leveraging these automated tools, you can optimize your training pipelines for large language models, ensuring robust performance, reproducibility, and efficient resource utilization. This comprehensive approach not only saves time and computational costs but also enables systematic exploration of the hyperparameter space, leading to better overall model performance.

Chapter 11: Evaluation and Performance Metrics

Evaluating large language models (LLMs) after fine-tuning is a critical step in ensuring that the model meets its intended goals. Effective evaluation involves both quantitative metrics—which provide objective, numerical assessments—and qualitative evaluations, which rely on human judgment to gauge factors such as coherence, fluency, and user satisfaction. This chapter provides a comprehensive overview of these evaluation methods, including detailed explanations, examples, and code snippets.

11.1 Quantitative Metrics: Accuracy, F1, BLEU, etc.

Quantitative metrics provide measurable insights into a model's performance. Depending on the task—whether it is classification, generation, or translation—different metrics are used to evaluate success.

Common Quantitative Metrics

1. **Classification Metrics:**
   - **Accuracy:**
     The proportion of correct predictions over the total number of predictions.
     Use Case: Suitable for balanced classification tasks.
   - **Precision and Recall:**
     - **Precision:** The proportion of true positive predictions among all positive predictions.
     - **Recall:** The proportion of true positives among all actual positive cases.
       Use Case: Useful when false positives or false negatives carry different costs.
   - **F1-Score:**
     The harmonic mean of precision and recall, providing a single score that balances both.
     Use Case: Especially useful for imbalanced datasets.
2. **Generation Metrics:**
   - **BLEU (Bilingual Evaluation Understudy):**
     Measures the overlap between the generated text and a reference text by comparing n-grams.
     Use Case: Common in machine translation.

- ○ **ROUGE (Recall-Oriented Understudy for Gisting Evaluation):**
  Evaluates the recall of n-grams between the generated and reference texts.
  Use Case: Often used for summarization tasks.
- ○ **METEOR:**
  Considers synonymy and stemming in addition to exact word matches.
  Use Case: Used in translation and summarization to capture more semantic similarity.

3. **Regression Metrics (for tasks predicting continuous values):**
   - ○ **Mean Squared Error (MSE):**
     The average squared difference between predicted and actual values.
   - ○ **Mean Absolute Error (MAE):**
     The average absolute difference between predicted and actual values.

Example: Evaluating a Fine-Tuned Classification Model

Below is an example that demonstrates how to calculate common classification metrics using the scikit-learn library in a fine-tuning scenario with a Hugging Face model.

python

```python
from transformers import AutoTokenizer, AutoModelForSequenceClassification, Trainer, TrainingArguments

from datasets import load_dataset

from sklearn.metrics import accuracy_score, precision_recall_fscore_support


# Load a pre-trained model and tokenizer for classification

model_name = "bert-base-uncased"

model = AutoModelForSequenceClassification.from_pretrained(model_name, num_labels=2)

tokenizer = AutoTokenizer.from_pretrained(model_name)
```

```python
# Load a dataset (using the IMDB dataset for sentiment analysis)

dataset = load_dataset("imdb")

# Use a subset for faster evaluation

test_dataset = dataset["test"].shuffle(seed=42).select(range(500))


# Tokenization function

def tokenize_function(examples):

    return tokenizer(examples["text"], padding="max_length",
truncation=True, max_length=128)


test_dataset = test_dataset.map(tokenize_function, batched=True)


# Define a function to compute metrics

def compute_metrics(eval_pred):

    logits, labels = eval_pred

    predictions = logits.argmax(axis=-1)

    accuracy = accuracy_score(labels, predictions)

    precision, recall, f1, _ = precision_recall_fscore_support(labels,
predictions, average="binary")

    return {

        "accuracy": accuracy,

        "precision": precision,

        "recall": recall,

        "f1": f1,
```

```
    }


# Define training arguments (only for evaluation in this example)
training_args = TrainingArguments(
    output_dir="./results",
    per_device_eval_batch_size=16,
    evaluation_strategy="epoch",
)


# Initialize the Trainer with the compute_metrics function
trainer = Trainer(
    model=model,
    args=training_args,
    eval_dataset=test_dataset,
    compute_metrics=compute_metrics,
)


# Evaluate the model
eval_results = trainer.evaluate()
print("Evaluation Metrics:")
print(eval_results)
```

Explanation:

- **Model and Tokenizer Loading:**
  We load a pre-trained BERT model and its corresponding tokenizer.
- **Dataset Preparation:**
  The IMDB test dataset is tokenized with consistent padding and truncation.
- **Metric Computation:**
  The compute_metrics function calculates accuracy, precision, recall, and F1-score using scikit-learn's functions.
- **Trainer API:**
  The Trainer API simplifies the evaluation process by handling data batching and metric computation.

Summary Table: Quantitative Metrics

Metric	Description	Common Use Case
Accuracy	Proportion of correct predictions.	Balanced classification tasks.
Precision	Proportion of true positives among predicted positives.	When false positives are costly.
Recall	Proportion of true positives among actual positives.	When false negatives are costly.
F1-Score	Harmonic mean of precision and recall.	Imbalanced classification.
BLEU	N-gram overlap between generated and reference text.	Machine translation.

ROUGE	Recall of n-grams between generated and reference text.	Summarization.
METEOR	Considers synonymy and stemming in text generation evaluation.	Translation, summarization.
MSE/MAE	Mean squared/absolute error for regression tasks.	Regression tasks.

11.2 Qualitative Evaluation: Human-in-the-Loop and User Studies

While quantitative metrics provide objective measures, they may not fully capture the nuances of language quality, such as coherence, relevance, and user satisfaction. Qualitative evaluation methods complement quantitative assessments by incorporating human judgment.

Human-in-the-Loop Evaluation

What It Involves:
Human-in-the-loop evaluation incorporates feedback from human evaluators at various stages of model development. This process can be iterative, with human reviewers assessing model outputs and providing feedback that is then used to refine the model.

Methods:

- **Expert Reviews:**
  Domain experts evaluate the model outputs for accuracy, coherence, and relevance. For instance, legal or medical experts might review documents generated by a fine-tuned model.
- **Crowdsourcing:**
  Platforms such as Amazon Mechanical Turk can be used to gather feedback from

a diverse pool of human evaluators on tasks like sentiment analysis or content generation.

- **Pairwise Comparisons:**
  Evaluators compare outputs from different models or different versions of the same model to determine which performs better according to specific criteria.

User Studies

What They Entail:
User studies involve real-world users interacting with the model in its intended application environment. Feedback is collected through surveys, interviews, or direct observation to assess usability, satisfaction, and overall impact.

Key Aspects:

- **Task-Based Evaluation:**
  Users perform specific tasks (e.g., asking questions, summarizing content) and then rate the quality of the model's outputs.
- **Qualitative Feedback:**
  Open-ended questions allow users to provide detailed insights into the strengths and weaknesses of the model.
- **Longitudinal Studies:**
  Tracking user satisfaction and performance over time can reveal improvements or degradations in model performance after updates or fine-tuning cycles.

Example: Conducting a Simple Human Evaluation

Below is an example of how you might structure a simple human evaluation for a text generation task using a survey format.

1. **Preparation:**
   - Select a sample of model outputs.
   - Develop a questionnaire with specific criteria (e.g., relevance, coherence, fluency, and informativeness).
2. **Survey Design (Pseudocode):**

plaintext

Questionnaire for Evaluating Generated Text:

----

1. How relevant is the generated text to the input prompt? (Scale: 1-5)

2. How coherent is the generated text? (Scale: 1-5)

3. How fluent and natural does the text sound? (Scale: 1-5)

4. Overall, how satisfied are you with the generated text? (Scale: 1-5)

5. Open-Ended Feedback: Please provide any additional comments.

----

3. **Collecting Feedback:**
   - Distribute the survey to a group of evaluators (could be internal experts or external users).
   - Aggregate the quantitative scores and analyze qualitative comments for recurring themes.

Summary Table: Qualitative Evaluation Methods

Method	Description	Benefits
Expert Reviews	Domain experts assess outputs based on specific criteria.	High reliability; domain-specific insights.
Crowdsourcing	A large number of evaluators provide feedback via online platforms.	Diverse perspectives; scalable feedback.
Pairwise Comparisons	Evaluators compare outputs from different models or model versions.	Direct comparative assessment; minimizes bias.

User Studies	Real-world users interact with the model and provide feedback.	Practical insights; measures user satisfaction.

Evaluating the performance of fine-tuned language models requires a balanced approach that incorporates both quantitative and qualitative assessments. Quantitative metrics—such as accuracy, F1-score, BLEU, and ROUGE—provide objective, numerical insights into model performance on specific tasks. However, qualitative evaluations, including human-in-the-loop assessments and user studies, capture subtler aspects of language quality that numbers alone cannot express.

By employing both types of evaluation methods, you can obtain a comprehensive understanding of your model's strengths and weaknesses, ensuring that it not only performs well on standard benchmarks but also meets the nuanced expectations of end users. The detailed examples, code snippets, and summary tables in this chapter provide a solid foundation for designing and implementing robust evaluation frameworks for your fine-tuned language models.

11.3 Robustness, Fairness, and Bias Evaluation

As language models are increasingly deployed in real-world applications, it is essential to evaluate them not only in terms of accuracy and performance but also for robustness, fairness, and bias. These aspects ensure that models are reliable, equitable, and do not propagate harmful stereotypes or discriminatory behavior. This section discusses methods to assess robustness against adversarial inputs, evaluate fairness across different demographic groups, and identify and mitigate biases present in model outputs.

Robustness Evaluation

Definition:
Robustness refers to a model's ability to maintain high performance when faced with noisy, adversarial, or unexpected inputs. A robust model should perform consistently across different scenarios, even when data quality varies.

Approaches to Evaluate Robustness:

1. **Adversarial Testing:**
   Introduce small perturbations or adversarial examples to the input text and assess how the model's predictions change. Techniques include:
   - Adding typos or synonyms.
   - Altering sentence structure.
   - Using adversarial attack libraries (e.g., TextAttack).
2. **Stress Testing:**
   Evaluate the model on challenging or out-of-distribution examples to observe performance drops.
3. **Robustness Metrics:**
   Metrics such as the adversarial accuracy (accuracy on adversarially perturbed data) can be used to quantify robustness.

Example: Evaluating Robustness with Adversarial Inputs

Below is a simplified example that demonstrates how to assess a model's robustness by introducing a common typo into the input text.

python

```python
import torch

from transformers import AutoTokenizer, AutoModelForSequenceClassification

from sklearn.metrics import accuracy_score


# Load a pre-trained model and tokenizer

model_name = "bert-base-uncased"

model = AutoModelForSequenceClassification.from_pretrained(model_name, num_labels=2)

tokenizer = AutoTokenizer.from_pretrained(model_name)


def predict(text):
```

```python
    inputs = tokenizer(text, return_tensors="pt", truncation=True,
padding=True, max_length=128)

    with torch.no_grad():

        outputs = model(**inputs)

    logits = outputs.logits

    prediction = logits.argmax(dim=-1).item()

    return prediction


# Original text and a perturbed version with a typo

original_text = "I absolutely loved the movie!"

perturbed_text = "I absolutley loved the movie!"  # 'absolutely' misspelled


original_prediction = predict(original_text)

perturbed_prediction = predict(perturbed_text)


print("Original Prediction:", original_prediction)

print("Perturbed Prediction:", perturbed_prediction)
```

Explanation:

- The example shows how a simple typo ("absolutley" vs. "absolutely") might affect model predictions.
- By comparing outputs on the original and perturbed texts, one can gauge the model's robustness to minor input variations.

Fairness and Bias Evaluation

Definition:

Fairness involves ensuring that a model's performance does not unduly favor or harm particular groups, while bias evaluation identifies systematic errors or prejudices present in the model's outputs.

Approaches to Evaluate Fairness and Bias:

1. **Disaggregated Performance Metrics:**
   Evaluate the model's performance separately for different demographic groups (e.g., gender, race, age) using metrics such as accuracy, precision, recall, and F1-score. Differences in these metrics may indicate bias.
2. **Bias Metrics:**
   Metrics such as Statistical Parity Difference, Equal Opportunity Difference, and Disparate Impact can quantify fairness.
   - *Example:* Compare false positive rates across groups.
3. **Qualitative Analysis:**
   Review outputs manually to identify biased language or stereotyping.
4. **Bias Mitigation Techniques:**
   Once biases are identified, techniques like re-sampling, re-weighting, adversarial debiasing, or post-processing corrections can be applied.

Example: Evaluating Fairness Using False Positive Rates

Below is an example that computes false positive rates for two hypothetical groups using scikit-learn.

python

```
import numpy as np


# Simulated true labels and predictions for two demographic groups: Group A and Group B

true_labels_A = np.array([0, 1, 0, 1, 0])

predictions_A = np.array([0, 1, 1, 1, 0])


true_labels_B = np.array([0, 1, 0, 1, 0])
```

```
predictions_B = np.array([1, 1, 0, 1, 1])


def false_positive_rate(true_labels, predictions):

    # Count false positives: predicted positive but actual negative

    false_positives = np.sum((predictions == 1) & (true_labels == 0))

    true_negatives = np.sum(true_labels == 0)

    return false_positives / true_negatives if true_negatives > 0 else 0


fpr_A = false_positive_rate(true_labels_A, predictions_A)

fpr_B = false_positive_rate(true_labels_B, predictions_B)


print("False Positive Rate for Group A:", fpr_A)

print("False Positive Rate for Group B:", fpr_B)


# A significant difference between fpr_A and fpr_B could indicate bias.
```

Explanation:

- The function calculates the false positive rate (FPR) for each group.
- Comparing FPRs across groups helps in detecting fairness issues; significant disparities may signal bias.

Summary Table: Robustness, Fairness, and Bias Evaluation

Aspect	Evaluation Approach	Key Metrics/Methods

Robustness	Adversarial testing, stress testing	Adversarial accuracy, performance on perturbed inputs
Fairness	Disaggregated performance evaluation	Accuracy, F1, precision, recall per demographic group
Bias	Quantitative bias metrics and qualitative reviews	Statistical Parity Difference, Equal Opportunity Difference, Disparate Impact

11.4 Continuous Monitoring and Model Drift

Once a model is deployed, continuous monitoring is essential to ensure that its performance remains stable over time. Model drift occurs when the model's performance degrades due to changes in the input data distribution or evolving external conditions.

Continuous Monitoring

Definition:
Continuous monitoring involves regularly evaluating the model's performance on new data and tracking key metrics over time.

Components:

1. **Automated Metric Logging:**
   Implement logging systems that automatically record metrics such as accuracy, loss, and other task-specific measures during production.
2. **Dashboards:**
   Visualization tools (e.g., Grafana, Weights & Biases) display trends and alert stakeholders to performance deviations.

3. **Alert Systems:**
   Set thresholds for key metrics; trigger alerts when performance drops below acceptable levels.

Example: Using Weights & Biases for Continuous Monitoring

python

```python
# Assume Weights & Biases is already integrated with training and deployment

import wandb


# Initialize W&B for a new run

wandb.init(project="llm-monitoring", entity="your-entity-name")


# During deployment, log evaluation metrics periodically

def log_metrics(metrics):

    wandb.log(metrics)


# Simulated periodic metric logging (in a real system, this would be part of a monitoring pipeline)

import time

for i in range(5):

    # Simulate metrics for demonstration

    simulated_metrics = {

        "accuracy": 0.85 - i * 0.01,  # Gradually decreasing accuracy

        "loss": 0.5 + i * 0.05,
```

```
}

log_metrics(simulated_metrics)

print(f"Logged metrics: {simulated_metrics}")

time.sleep(1)  # Simulate time delay between evaluations
```

Explanation:

- The code demonstrates how to log metrics to Weights & Biases in a loop, simulating continuous monitoring.
- In production, this process would be automated and integrated with real-time data.

Model Drift

Definition:
Model drift refers to the deterioration of model performance over time due to shifts in the data distribution or changes in the environment.

Types of Drift:

1. **Concept Drift:**
   Changes in the underlying relationship between input data and target labels.
2. **Data Drift:**
   Changes in the input data distribution, even if the underlying relationship remains the same.

Detection and Mitigation:

- **Regular Evaluation:**
  Continuously evaluate the model on fresh data to detect deviations.
- **Statistical Tests:**
  Use statistical methods (e.g., Kolmogorov–Smirnov test) to detect changes in data distributions.
- **Retraining or Fine-Tuning:**
  When significant drift is detected, retrain or further fine-tune the model on new data.

- **Feedback Loops:**
  Incorporate user feedback and human-in-the-loop evaluations to adjust for drift.

Example: Detecting Data Drift with a Statistical Test

Below is an example using the Kolmogorov–Smirnov (KS) test from the SciPy library to compare the distributions of a feature from two different time periods.

python

```python
import numpy as np

from scipy.stats import ks_2samp


# Simulated data: feature distributions from two time periods

data_period1 = np.random.normal(loc=0.0, scale=1.0, size=1000)

data_period2 = np.random.normal(loc=0.2, scale=1.1, size=1000)  # Slight drift in mean and scale


# Perform the KS test

ks_statistic, p_value = ks_2samp(data_period1, data_period2)


print("KS Statistic:", ks_statistic)

print("P-Value:", p_value)


if p_value < 0.05:

    print("Significant drift detected.")

else:

    print("No significant drift detected.")
```

Explanation:

- The KS test compares the empirical distributions of two samples.
- A low p-value indicates that the distributions differ significantly, suggesting data drift.

Summary Table: Continuous Monitoring and Model Drift

Aspect	Description	Key Tools/Methods
Continuous Monitoring	Regular evaluation of model performance and logging of key metrics.	Automated logging, dashboards, alert systems.
Model Drift	Deterioration of performance due to changes in data distribution or relationships.	Regular re-evaluation, statistical tests, retraining strategies.

Evaluating robustness, fairness, and bias is critical to ensuring that language models are not only accurate but also reliable and equitable. Quantitative and qualitative evaluations help detect vulnerabilities and disparities in model performance. Moreover, continuous monitoring and proactive detection of model drift are essential for maintaining the long-term efficacy of deployed models. By integrating automated monitoring tools and statistical methods, organizations can respond quickly to performance degradation and ensure that models continue to perform optimally in dynamic environments.

The detailed explanations, code examples, and summary tables provided in this chapter equip you with practical strategies to implement robust evaluation frameworks and maintain high-quality performance over the lifecycle of your language models.

Chapter 12: Scaling Fine-Tuning Operations

As the size of language models and datasets increases, scaling fine-tuning operations becomes essential for reducing training time and handling large workloads. In this chapter, we discuss strategies and techniques to scale your fine-tuning operations effectively. We cover distributed training techniques that allow you to leverage multiple GPUs or machines, and we explore how to utilize cloud platforms and GPU clusters to maximize computational resources.

12.1 Distributed Training Techniques

Distributed training is a method of splitting a training job across multiple devices—such as GPUs or nodes—to speed up computation and manage larger models and datasets. Two primary forms of distributed training are data parallelism and model parallelism.

Data Parallelism

Concept:
Data parallelism involves replicating the model across multiple GPUs and dividing the training data into mini-batches that are processed in parallel. Each GPU computes gradients on its portion of data, and then gradients are aggregated to update the shared model parameters.

Key Points:

- **Synchronous Training:**
  All GPUs update the model simultaneously after each mini-batch. Frameworks like PyTorch's DistributedDataParallel (DDP) ensure that gradients are averaged across GPUs.
- **Scalability:**
  Data parallelism scales well when the model fits into a single GPU's memory, as the workload is divided across multiple devices.

Example: DistributedDataParallel in PyTorch

Below is an example of how to set up distributed training using PyTorch's DistributedDataParallel (DDP).

python

```python
import os

import torch

import torch.nn as nn

import torch.optim as optim

import torch.distributed as dist

from torch.nn.parallel import DistributedDataParallel as DDP

from torch.utils.data import DataLoader, DistributedSampler,
TensorDataset


def setup(rank, world_size):

    # Initialize the distributed process group

    dist.init_process_group("nccl", rank=rank, world_size=world_size)


def cleanup():

    dist.destroy_process_group()


def main(rank, world_size):

    setup(rank, world_size)


    # Create a simple model

    model = nn.Linear(10, 2).to(rank)

    ddp_model = DDP(model, device_ids=[rank])


    # Generate dummy data and create DataLoader with DistributedSampler
```

```python
x = torch.randn(1000, 10)

y = torch.randint(0, 2, (1000,))

dataset = TensorDataset(x, y)

sampler = DistributedSampler(dataset, num_replicas=world_size,
rank=rank)

dataloader = DataLoader(dataset, batch_size=32, sampler=sampler)


criterion = nn.CrossEntropyLoss()

optimizer = optim.Adam(ddp_model.parameters(), lr=0.001)


# Training loop
for epoch in range(5):
    sampler.set_epoch(epoch)
    for batch_x, batch_y in dataloader:
        batch_x = batch_x.to(rank)
        batch_y = batch_y.to(rank)
        optimizer.zero_grad()
        outputs = ddp_model(batch_x)
        loss = criterion(outputs, batch_y)
        loss.backward()
        optimizer.step()
    print(f"Rank {rank}, Epoch {epoch+1}, Loss: {loss.item()}")


cleanup()
```

```
if __name__ == "__main__":

    world_size = 2  # Number of GPUs/nodes

    # Use torch.multiprocessing.spawn to launch distributed processes

    torch.multiprocessing.spawn(main, args=(world_size,),
nprocs=world_size, join=True)
```

Explanation:

- **Distributed Process Group:**
  The setup function initializes a process group using the NCCL backend (optimal for GPUs).
- **Model Replication:**
  The model is wrapped with DistributedDataParallel so that it is replicated across multiple GPUs.
- **DataLoader with DistributedSampler:**
  The DistributedSampler ensures that each process gets a unique portion of the data.
- **Training Loop:**
  Each GPU computes its local loss and gradients, which are then averaged during the backward pass.
- **Cleanup:**
  The distributed process group is destroyed after training.

Model Parallelism

Concept:
Model parallelism divides the model itself across multiple GPUs. This approach is useful when the model is too large to fit into the memory of a single GPU. Each GPU handles a part of the model, and intermediate outputs are communicated between GPUs.

Considerations:

- **Communication Overhead:**
  Splitting a model across GPUs introduces communication overhead, which may affect training speed.

- **Complexity:**
  Model parallelism requires careful partitioning of the model and managing data transfers between GPUs.

Summary Table: Distributed Training Techniques

Technique	Concept	Pros	Cons
Data Parallelism	Replicates the model on multiple GPUs; splits the data among them.	Simple implementation; scales well when model fits in one GPU.	Requires efficient gradient synchronization.
Model Parallelism	Splits the model itself across multiple GPUs.	Enables training of models too large for a single GPU.	Higher communication overhead; more complex.

12.2 Utilizing Cloud Platforms and GPU Clusters

Leveraging cloud platforms and GPU clusters is an effective way to scale fine-tuning operations without investing in expensive on-premise hardware. Cloud services provide flexible, scalable, and on-demand access to high-performance computing resources.

Cloud Platforms for Distributed Training

Popular Cloud Platforms:

- **Amazon Web Services (AWS):**
  AWS offers EC2 instances with GPU support (e.g., p3 and p4 instances) and managed services like SageMaker for machine learning workflows.
- **Google Cloud Platform (GCP):**
  GCP provides Compute Engine instances with GPUs and services such as AI Platform for scalable machine learning operations.

- **Microsoft Azure:**
  Azure offers virtual machines with GPU capabilities and the Azure Machine Learning service for orchestrating training jobs.

Utilizing GPU Clusters

Key Considerations:

- **Cluster Setup:**
  Cloud platforms allow you to set up GPU clusters where multiple GPUs can be orchestrated across several nodes. This setup is ideal for distributed training jobs.
- **Job Scheduling:**
  Use job scheduling systems (e.g., Kubernetes, SLURM) or cloud-specific orchestration tools to manage training jobs and resources effectively.
- **Cost Management:**
  Cloud platforms typically charge by the hour for GPU usage. Utilize spot instances or preemptible VMs to reduce costs, but be mindful of potential interruptions.

Example: Launching a Distributed Training Job on AWS Using SageMaker

Below is a high-level example of configuring a distributed training job using Amazon SageMaker with PyTorch.

python

```python
import sagemaker

from sagemaker.pytorch import PyTorch


# Define the entry point for the training script

entry_point = "train.py"  # Your training script with distributed training code (similar to DDP example)


# Define the PyTorch estimator with distributed training settings

estimator = PyTorch(
```

```python
    entry_point=entry_point,

    role="SageMakerRole",  # Replace with your SageMaker execution role

    framework_version="1.8.0",

    py_version="py3",

    instance_count=2,  # Number of instances (GPUs across nodes)

    instance_type="ml.p3.2xlarge",  # Instance type with GPU support

    hyperparameters={

        "epochs": 5,

        "batch_size": 32,

        "learning_rate": 2e-5,

    },

)


# Launch the training job

estimator.fit({"train": "s3://your-bucket/train/", "test": "s3://your-bucket/test/"})
```

Explanation:

- **SageMaker PyTorch Estimator:**
  The estimator encapsulates all necessary configurations for distributed training on AWS.
- **Instance Settings:**
  The instance count and type determine the GPU resources allocated for the job.
- **Hyperparameters and Data Channels:**
  Hyperparameters are passed to the training script, and data is specified via S3 channels.

- **Job Submission:**
  The .fit() method launches the training job on the specified cluster, handling distributed setup automatically.

Summary Table: Cloud Platforms and GPU Clusters

Platform/Tool	Key Features	Use Cases
AWS (EC2, SageMaker)	Wide range of GPU instances; managed ML services; robust ecosystem.	Scalable training, production deployments, experiment tracking.
Google Cloud (Compute Engine, AI Platform)	Flexible GPU instances; integrated AI services; cost-effective with preemptible VMs.	Research experiments, large-scale distributed training.
Microsoft Azure	GPU-enabled VMs; Azure Machine Learning service; strong enterprise integration.	Enterprise-level ML projects, scalable pipelines.
Kubernetes/SLURM	Open-source orchestration tools for managing clusters.	Custom cluster management, distributed training orchestration.

Scaling fine-tuning operations is crucial for handling large language models and vast datasets. Distributed training techniques, such as data parallelism and model parallelism, allow you to split the workload across multiple GPUs or nodes, thereby accelerating training and managing memory constraints. Additionally, leveraging cloud platforms and GPU clusters provides flexible, on-demand resources, making it easier to run large-scale experiments and production deployments.

By integrating robust distributed training techniques and cloud solutions into your fine-tuning workflow, you can efficiently scale your operations while maintaining high performance and managing costs. The detailed code examples, tables, and explanations provided in this chapter serve as a practical guide for implementing these strategies in real-world scenarios.

12.3 Data Parallelism vs. Model Parallelism

When scaling fine-tuning operations for large language models (LLMs), distributed training techniques are essential. Two primary approaches are data parallelism and model parallelism. Each method addresses different challenges and has its own benefits and trade-offs. This section explains both approaches, highlights their differences, and provides examples to help you determine which strategy best suits your training needs.

Data Parallelism

Definition:
Data parallelism involves replicating the entire model on multiple GPUs or nodes and splitting the input data among these devices. Each device computes the forward and backward passes on its own mini-batch, and the gradients are then aggregated (typically via an all-reduce operation) to update the shared model parameters.

Key Characteristics:

- **Model Replication:**
  The model is duplicated across all available devices.
- **Gradient Aggregation:**
  After processing each mini-batch, gradients from all devices are averaged or summed before updating the model.
- **Scalability:**
  Effective when the model fits entirely on each device's memory.
- **Ease of Implementation:**
  Frameworks such as PyTorch's DistributedDataParallel (DDP) make data parallelism straightforward to implement.

Advantages:

- Simple to implement if the model fits on each GPU.
- Scales linearly with the number of GPUs for many tasks.

- Minimal modifications required to existing training code.

Disadvantages:

- Memory constraints: All devices must have enough memory to store a copy of the entire model.
- Communication overhead: Aggregating gradients across many devices can become a bottleneck, especially as the number of GPUs increases.

Model Parallelism

Definition:
Model parallelism splits the model itself across multiple GPUs. Different parts of the model are hosted on different devices, and data flows sequentially through the split model parts. This is particularly useful when the model is too large to fit on a single GPU.

Key Characteristics:

- **Model Partitioning:**
  The model's layers or components are divided among GPUs.
- **Inter-Device Communication:**
  Intermediate outputs must be communicated between GPUs as data flows through the model.
- **Scalability:**
  Enables training of very large models that exceed the memory capacity of a single GPU.
- **Complexity:**
  Requires careful partitioning of the model and management of communication overhead.

Advantages:

- Allows training of models larger than a single GPU's memory.
- Can be combined with data parallelism for further scalability (hybrid parallelism).

Disadvantages:

- Increased communication overhead due to frequent data transfers between devices.
- More complex to implement and optimize compared to data parallelism.

- Load balancing issues: Ensuring that all GPUs are equally utilized can be challenging.

Comparative Summary

Below is a table summarizing the differences between data parallelism and model parallelism:

Aspect	Data Parallelism	Model Parallelism
Concept	Replicates the entire model on each device and splits the data.	Splits the model itself across multiple devices.
When to Use	When the model fits in one GPU's memory; scaling with more data.	When the model is too large for a single GPU's memory.
Implementation Complexity	Relatively simple (using tools like DDP).	More complex; requires partitioning and managing inter-GPU communication.
Communication Overhead	Moderate (synchronizing gradients after each mini-batch).	High (frequent transfers of intermediate results between GPUs).

Scalability	Scales well if communication is efficient and model fits in memory.	Enables training of extremely large models; may need hybrid strategies.

Code Example: Data Parallelism with DistributedDataParallel (DDP)

Below is a complete example that demonstrates how to implement data parallelism using PyTorch's DistributedDataParallel (DDP).

python

```python
import os

import torch

import torch.nn as nn

import torch.optim as optim

import torch.distributed as dist

from torch.nn.parallel import DistributedDataParallel as DDP

from torch.utils.data import DataLoader, DistributedSampler, TensorDataset


def setup(rank, world_size):
    # Initialize the distributed environment.
    dist.init_process_group("nccl", rank=rank, world_size=world_size)


def cleanup():
    dist.destroy_process_group()
```

```python
def main(rank, world_size):
    setup(rank, world_size)

    # Create a simple model.
    model = nn.Linear(10, 2).to(rank)
    ddp_model = DDP(model, device_ids=[rank])

    # Create dummy dataset.
    x = torch.randn(1000, 10)
    y = torch.randint(0, 2, (1000,))
    dataset = TensorDataset(x, y)

    # Use DistributedSampler to split data among GPUs.
    sampler = DistributedSampler(dataset, num_replicas=world_size, rank=rank)
    dataloader = DataLoader(dataset, batch_size=32, sampler=sampler)

    criterion = nn.CrossEntropyLoss()
    optimizer = optim.Adam(ddp_model.parameters(), lr=0.001)

    # Training loop.
    for epoch in range(5):
        sampler.set_epoch(epoch)
```

```python
    for batch_x, batch_y in dataloader:

        batch_x = batch_x.to(rank)

        batch_y = batch_y.to(rank)

        optimizer.zero_grad()

        outputs = ddp_model(batch_x)

        loss = criterion(outputs, batch_y)

        loss.backward()

        optimizer.step()

    print(f"Rank {rank}, Epoch {epoch+1}, Loss: {loss.item()}")


    cleanup()


if __name__ == "__main__":

    world_size = 2  # Number of GPUs

    torch.multiprocessing.spawn(main, args=(world_size,),
nprocs=world_size, join=True)
```

Explanation:

- **Setup and Cleanup:**
  The setup function initializes the NCCL-based distributed process group, and cleanup terminates it after training.
- **Model Replication:**
  The model is wrapped in DistributedDataParallel to synchronize gradients across GPUs.
- **DataLoader:**
  A DistributedSampler ensures that each GPU processes a unique subset of data.

- **Training Loop:**
  Each GPU independently computes its gradients, which are then averaged across all GPUs.

12.4 Case Studies on Scaling in Production

In production environments, scaling fine-tuning operations is crucial for handling large-scale deployments and ensuring robust performance. This section presents real-world case studies and practical examples that illustrate how organizations have successfully scaled their fine-tuning operations.

Case Study 1: Scaling Fine-Tuning for a Customer Support Chatbot

Background:
A company developed a customer support chatbot using a pre-trained language model. The initial fine-tuning was performed on a single GPU, but as usage increased, the company faced the challenge of handling a large volume of interactions and continuously updating the model with new data.

Approach:

- **Data Parallelism:**
  The company implemented data parallelism using PyTorch's DistributedDataParallel (DDP) to train on multiple GPUs. This reduced training time significantly and allowed the model to be updated more frequently.
- **Automated Pipeline:**
  They integrated automated hyperparameter tuning and continuous evaluation with cloud-based GPU clusters (AWS SageMaker), ensuring that model updates did not disrupt production.
- **Outcome:**
  The chatbot's performance improved, with faster response times and more accurate answers. The scalable training pipeline enabled daily model updates and seamless integration with customer support systems.

Case Study 2: Fine-Tuning for a Multi-Domain Legal Document Analyzer

Background:
A legal tech firm needed to fine-tune a large language model for classifying and summarizing legal documents across multiple domains (e.g., contracts, court opinions, legal briefs).

Approach:

- **Model Parallelism and Hybrid Parallelism:**
  The legal documents required a model too large to fit on a single GPU. The firm employed model parallelism to split the model across several GPUs and combined this with data parallelism to process large volumes of data.
- **Cloud-Based Infrastructure:**
  The firm utilized Google Cloud's AI Platform to run distributed training jobs, leveraging preemptible VMs to reduce costs while maintaining high computational throughput.
- **Outcome:**
  The multi-domain legal document analyzer achieved state-of-the-art accuracy while processing thousands of documents per day. The hybrid parallelism strategy allowed the firm to scale the model efficiently without compromising on performance or incurring prohibitive costs.

Case Study 3: Scaling a Multi-Lingual Translation Service

Background:
A translation service provider wanted to fine-tune a transformer-based model for multiple language pairs. Given the diversity of languages and the volume of data, the service needed a robust scaling strategy.

Approach:

- **Distributed Training with Cloud GPU Clusters:**
  The provider set up a distributed training pipeline using Microsoft Azure's GPU clusters. They leveraged both data parallelism (to handle vast amounts of parallel translation data) and model parallelism (to support a large multilingual transformer model).
- **Resource Management and Monitoring:**
  The system incorporated continuous monitoring of training metrics and automatic checkpointing to ensure stability and quick recovery from failures.
- **Outcome:**
  The translation service improved its throughput and accuracy, offering real-time translations across multiple language pairs. The scalable infrastructure allowed for rapid model updates and adaptation to new languages as demand grew.

Summary Table: Scaling in Production

Case Study	Challenge	Approach	Outcome

Customer Support Chatbot	High volume of interactions; frequent model updates.	Data parallelism with DDP; automated cloud-based training.	Faster updates; improved performance and response time.
Legal Document Analyzer	Large, multi-domain model exceeding single-GPU memory.	Hybrid parallelism (model + data parallelism); cloud infrastructure.	State-of-the-art accuracy; scalable processing of diverse legal texts.
Multi-Lingual Translation Service	Handling multiple language pairs and massive datasets.	Distributed training on cloud GPU clusters; resource monitoring.	Real-time, accurate translations; flexible scaling for new languages.

Scaling fine-tuning operations is essential for leveraging the full potential of large language models in production environments. Data parallelism and model parallelism offer distinct methods to distribute the training workload, each with its own advantages and challenges. Through practical case studies, we have seen how organizations overcome real-world challenges by combining these techniques with cloud platforms, automated pipelines, and robust resource management strategies.

By understanding the trade-offs between data and model parallelism and learning from production examples, you can design scalable fine-tuning operations that meet the demands of large-scale deployments while ensuring efficient use of computational resources and maintaining high model performance.

Chapter 13: Deployment and Integration

Once your language model has been fine-tuned to achieve excellent performance on your target tasks, the next critical step is deploying it for production use. Deployment involves converting your model into a format suitable for production environments, optimizing it for speed and efficiency, and then integrating it into applications via APIs or microservices. This chapter covers two major aspects: exporting and optimizing models for production, and serving models with APIs and microservices.

13.1 Exporting and Optimizing Models for Production

Deploying a model in production requires that it runs efficiently and reliably under real-world conditions. This often involves converting the model to a format that can be easily loaded in production environments and applying various optimizations to reduce latency and resource consumption.

Key Steps in Exporting and Optimizing Models

1. **Model Export:**
   The first step is to export the fine-tuned model into a format that can be loaded and executed outside the training environment. Common export formats include:
   - **TorchScript:** A way to serialize PyTorch models into an intermediate representation that can run independently from Python.
   - **ONNX (Open Neural Network Exchange):** A format that allows the model to be used in various frameworks and runtime environments.
   - **SavedModel (TensorFlow):** For TensorFlow models, the SavedModel format is widely used.
2. **Model Optimization:**
   After export, you can optimize the model to improve inference speed and reduce resource usage. Techniques include:
   - **Quantization:** Reducing the precision of model weights (e.g., from float32 to int8) to decrease model size and increase inference speed.
   - **Pruning:** Removing redundant or less important model parameters.
   - **Graph Optimization:** Tools such as ONNX Runtime or NVIDIA's TensorRT can further optimize the computation graph for faster execution.
3. **Benchmarking:**
   Measure the inference latency, throughput, and resource usage (CPU, GPU, memory) to ensure that the model meets production requirements.

Example: Exporting a PyTorch Model with TorchScript

Below is an example that demonstrates how to export a fine-tuned PyTorch model to TorchScript and then optimize it for production.

python

```python
import torch

from transformers import AutoModelForSequenceClassification, AutoTokenizer


# Load the fine-tuned model and tokenizer

model_name = "bert-base-uncased"

model = AutoModelForSequenceClassification.from_pretrained(model_name, num_labels=2)

tokenizer = AutoTokenizer.from_pretrained(model_name)


# Set the model to evaluation mode

model.eval()


# Examplc input to trace the model

dummy_input = tokenizer("This is an example.", return_tensors="pt")["input_ids"]


# Export the model using torch.jit.trace

traced_model = torch.jit.trace(model, dummy_input)
```

```
# Save the TorchScript model

traced_model.save("traced_model.pt")

print("Model exported as TorchScript successfully.")
```

Explanation:

- **Evaluation Mode:**
  Setting the model to evaluation mode (model.eval()) ensures that layers like dropout behave correctly during inference.
- **Tracing:**
  torch.jit.trace records the operations performed by the model on a sample input, producing a TorchScript version of the model.
- **Saving:**
  The model is saved to disk as a .pt file, which can later be loaded for fast, standalone inference.

Summary Table: Exporting and Optimizing Models

Step	Description	Tools/Formats
Model Export	Convert the trained model into a production-ready format.	TorchScript, ONNX, SavedModel
Quantization	Reduce model precision to decrease size and speed up inference.	PyTorch quantization toolkit, ONNX Runtime

Pruning	Remove redundant parameters to streamline the model.	PyTorch pruning APIs, third-party libraries
Graph Optimization	Optimize the computation graph for faster execution.	ONNX Runtime, NVIDIA TensorRT
Benchmarking	Measure performance metrics such as latency and throughput to ensure production viability.	Custom benchmarking scripts, profiler tools

13.2 Serving Models with APIs and Microservices

After exporting and optimizing your model, the next step is to integrate it into a production system. This is commonly achieved by serving the model through an API or as part of a microservice architecture. This approach makes it easy for various applications to send requests to the model and receive responses in real time.

Key Concepts in Model Serving

1. **API-Based Serving:**
   Create an API endpoint that accepts input data, passes it to the model for inference, and returns the output. This is often implemented using web frameworks such as FastAPI, Flask, or Django.
2. **Microservices Architecture:**
   Deploy the model as a microservice, a small, independent service that can be scaled, updated, and managed separately from the rest of the application.
3. **Containerization:**
   Using containers (e.g., Docker) helps encapsulate the model and its dependencies, ensuring consistency across different deployment environments.

4. **Scalability and Load Balancing:**
   In production, you may need to scale your model serving to handle high volumes of requests. Tools like Kubernetes can manage scaling and load balancing across multiple instances.

Example: Serving a Model with FastAPI

Below is an example of how to serve a TorchScript model using FastAPI. This example creates a simple API that accepts text input, tokenizes it, performs inference with the model, and returns the predicted label.

python

```python
from fastapi import FastAPI, HTTPException

import torch

from transformers import AutoTokenizer

import uvicorn


app = FastAPI()


# Load the exported TorchScript model and tokenizer

model = torch.jit.load("traced_model.pt")

tokenizer = AutoTokenizer.from_pretrained("bert-base-uncased")


# Ensure the model is in evaluation mode

model.eval()


@app.post("/predict")

async def predict(text: str):
```

```python
    if not text:

        raise HTTPException(status_code=400, detail="Input text is required.")


    # Tokenize the input text

    inputs = tokenizer(text, return_tensors="pt", padding="max_length", truncation=True, max_length=128)


    # Perform inference

    with torch.no_grad():

        outputs = model(inputs["input_ids"])


    # Get the predicted class (assuming binary classification)

    predicted_class = torch.argmax(outputs.logits, dim=-1).item()


    return {"predicted_class": predicted_class}


if __name__ == "__main__":

    uvicorn.run(app, host="0.0.0.0", port=8000)
```

Explanation:

- **FastAPI Initialization:**
  An instance of FastAPI is created to define the API endpoints.
- **Model Loading:**
  The TorchScript model is loaded using torch.jit.load, and the tokenizer is also initialized.

- **Prediction Endpoint:**
  The /predict endpoint receives a text string, tokenizes it, and performs inference with the model. The predicted class is extracted from the model's output.
- **Serving:**
  Uvicorn is used to run the API server, making the model accessible on port 8000.

Summary Table: Serving Models with APIs and Microservices

Aspect	Description	Tools/Technologies
API-Based Serving	Creating endpoints to accept input and return predictions in real time.	FastAPI, Flask, Django
Microservices Architecture	Deploying the model as an independent service that can scale and update separately.	Docker, Kubernetes, AWS Lambda
Containerization	Packaging the model and its dependencies into a container for consistent deployment.	Docker, Docker Compose, Kubernetes
Scalability	Managing high request volumes through load balancing and auto-scaling.	Kubernetes, AWS ECS/EKS, Google Kubernetes Engine (GKE)

Deploying and integrating fine-tuned language models into production involves exporting and optimizing the model, followed by serving it through robust APIs or microservices. Exporting the model using formats such as TorchScript or ONNX, combined with optimization techniques like quantization and pruning, ensures that the model is efficient and reliable for production use. Serving the model using API frameworks like FastAPI or integrating it into a microservices architecture provides the flexibility and scalability required for real-world applications.

By following the strategies and examples provided in this chapter, you can successfully transition from fine-tuning a model in a research environment to deploying it in production, ensuring that your model is both performant and accessible to end users in a scalable manner.

13.3 Real-Time Inference vs. Batch Processing

When deploying models in production, one of the key decisions is how to serve the model's predictions: as real-time responses or in batch mode. Both approaches have distinct advantages and use cases, and selecting the right strategy depends on the application's requirements, latency constraints, throughput needs, and infrastructure.

Real-Time Inference

Definition:
Real-time inference (or online inference) refers to the process of making predictions immediately upon receiving an input. This is essential for applications where rapid response times are critical, such as interactive chatbots, recommendation systems, or fraud detection.

Key Characteristics:

- **Low Latency:**
  The system is optimized to provide near-instantaneous responses.
- **Scalability:**
  The service must handle unpredictable or variable loads with minimal delay.
- **Stateless Requests:**
  Each prediction is typically independent, meaning the server processes one request at a time and returns the result immediately.

Advantages:

- **User Experience:**
  Real-time responses improve the user experience by providing immediate feedback.

- **Interactive Applications:**
  Essential for services where the model is part of an interactive workflow.

Challenges:

- **Infrastructure Complexity:**
  Requires low-latency networking, load balancing, and potentially autoscaling mechanisms.
- **Resource Utilization:**
  Must be optimized to handle peak loads without excessive resource consumption during idle periods.

Example: Real-Time Inference with FastAPI

Below is an example using FastAPI to serve a model for real-time inference:

python

```python
from fastapi import FastAPI, HTTPException

import torch

from transformers import AutoTokenizer

import uvicorn


app = FastAPI()


# Load the pre-trained model and tokenizer (using a TorchScript model for faster inference)

model = torch.jit.load("traced_model.pt")

tokenizer = AutoTokenizer.from_pretrained("bert-base-uncased")


# Ensure the model is in evaluation mode
```

```python
model.eval()


@app.post("/predict")
async def predict(text: str):
    if not text:
        raise HTTPException(status_code=400, detail="Input text is
required.")


    # Tokenize the input text
    inputs = tokenizer(text, return_tensors="pt", padding="max_length",
truncation=True, max_length=128)


    # Perform inference
    with torch.no_grad():
        outputs = model(inputs["input_ids"])


    # Get the predicted class (assuming binary classification)
    predicted_class = torch.argmax(outputs.logits, dim=-1).item()


    return {"predicted_class": predicted_class}

if __name__ == "__main__":
    uvicorn.run(app, host="0.0.0.0", port=8000)
```

Explanation:

- The FastAPI server defines a /predict endpoint.
- Each request is processed immediately: the input text is tokenized, passed to the model, and the result is returned.
- This setup ensures low latency and is well-suited for interactive applications.

Batch Processing

Definition:
Batch processing involves handling multiple inputs collectively in a batch, typically in an offline or scheduled manner. This approach is beneficial when real-time response is not critical, and throughput and cost efficiency are the main concerns.

Key Characteristics:

- **High Throughput:**
  Processing large volumes of data simultaneously.
- **Cost Efficiency:**
  Batch processing can be scheduled during off-peak hours to minimize costs.
- **Non-Interactive:**
  Outputs are generated in bulk and may be stored or used for further analysis rather than immediate display.

Advantages:

- **Efficient Resource Use:**
  Optimizes GPU/CPU utilization by processing data in parallel.
- **Data Analysis and Reporting:**
  Ideal for generating periodic reports, updating search indexes, or retraining models.

Challenges:

- **Latency:**
  Not suitable for applications that require immediate responses.
- **Scheduling Complexity:**
  Requires job schedulers and batch processing pipelines, which can add complexity to the system.

Example: Batch Processing with a Python Script

Below is a simplified example of batch processing where a model is applied to a dataset, and predictions are saved to a file.

python

```python
import torch

import pandas as pd

from transformers import AutoTokenizer

from tqdm import tqdm


# Load the TorchScript model and tokenizer

model = torch.jit.load("traced_model.pt")

tokenizer = AutoTokenizer.from_pretrained("bert-base-uncased")

model.eval()


# Load a CSV file containing multiple input texts

data = pd.read_csv("batch_input.csv")  # Assume the CSV has a column 'text'

predictions = []


# Process data in batches

batch_size = 32

for i in tqdm(range(0, len(data), batch_size)):

    batch_texts = data['text'].iloc[i:i+batch_size].tolist()

    inputs = tokenizer(batch_texts, return_tensors="pt", padding=True, truncation=True, max_length=128)
```

```python
with torch.no_grad():

    outputs = model(inputs["input_ids"])


batch_preds = torch.argmax(outputs.logits, dim=-1).tolist()

predictions.extend(batch_preds)


# Save predictions to a new CSV file

data['predicted_class'] = predictions

data.to_csv("batch_output.csv", index=False)

print("Batch processing complete. Predictions saved to batch_output.csv")
```

Explanation:

- The script processes a CSV file containing multiple text entries.
- Data is processed in batches, and predictions are generated for each batch.
- The predictions are saved back to a CSV file, making this approach suitable for non-real-time tasks like reporting.

Summary Table: Real-Time Inference vs. Batch Processing

Aspect	Real-Time Inference	Batch Processing
Latency	Very low; immediate response required.	Higher; outputs generated periodically.

Throughput	Optimized for individual, interactive requests.	Optimized for processing large volumes of data simultaneously.
Use Cases	Chatbots, recommendation systems, fraud detection.	Reporting, data analysis, offline processing, retraining.
Resource Utilization	Requires highly available, low-latency infrastructure.	Can be scheduled during off-peak hours for cost efficiency.
Complexity	Requires robust APIs, load balancing, and autoscaling.	Requires batch job schedulers and data pipelines.

13.4 Integrating with Existing Systems and Applications

Integrating a fine-tuned model into an existing technology stack is essential for delivering its capabilities to end users. This process involves ensuring seamless interaction between the model and other systems, such as web applications, databases, and external services.

Key Considerations for Integration

1. **API Design and Standardization:**
   - **RESTful APIs:**
     Expose model inference as a REST API to allow applications to interact with the model over HTTP.

- **GraphQL:**
  An alternative API design that can provide more flexibility in querying data, particularly when the client requires only specific fields.
- **Versioning:**
  Implement API versioning to ensure backward compatibility and smooth transitions when models are updated.

2. **Microservices Architecture:**
   - **Containerization:**
     Package the model and its serving infrastructure using Docker. This encapsulation ensures consistency across different environments.
   - **Service Discovery and Load Balancing:**
     Use tools like Kubernetes or Docker Swarm to manage microservices, scale instances, and balance incoming requests.
   - **Resilience and Monitoring:**
     Implement health checks, logging, and monitoring to quickly identify and resolve issues in production.

3. **Data Integration and Workflow Orchestration:**
   - **Integration with Databases:**
     Ensure that predictions can be stored and retrieved efficiently, either by writing to a database or integrating with a data warehouse.
   - **Message Queues:**
     For asynchronous processing or high-throughput environments, use message queues (e.g., Kafka, RabbitMQ) to decouple model inference from other application components.
   - **Workflow Orchestration:**
     Tools like Apache Airflow or Prefect can be used to schedule and manage end-to-end data processing pipelines that include model inference.

Example: Integrating a Model API into a Web Application

Below is an example of how a Flask-based web application might call a model API to display predictions on a webpage.

Model API (served via FastAPI as shown previously):

Assume the FastAPI model API is running at http://localhost:8000/predict.

Flask Web Application Code:

python

```python
from flask import Flask, request, render_template, jsonify
import requests


app = Flask(__name__)


# Home page with a form to submit text for prediction
@app.route("/", methods=["GET", "POST"])
def index():
    if request.method == "POST":
        text = request.form.get("text")
        # Call the model API for prediction
        response = requests.post("http://localhost:8000/predict",
json={"text": text})
        if response.status_code == 200:
            result = response.json()
            predicted_class = result.get("predicted_class")
        else:
            predicted_class = "Error: Unable to get prediction."
        return render_template("index.html", text=text,
predicted_class=predicted_class)
    return render_template("index.html", text="", predicted_class="")


if __name__ == "__main__":
    app.run(debug=True, port=5000)
```

index.html Template Example:

html

```
<!DOCTYPE html>
<html>
<head>
  <title>Model Prediction</title>
</head>
<body>
  <h1>Enter Text for Prediction</h1>
  <form method="post">
    <textarea name="text" rows="4" cols="50" placeholder="Enter text here..."></textarea><br><br>
    <input type="submit" value="Predict">
  </form>
  {% if predicted_class %}
    <h2>Predicted Class: {{ predicted_class }}</h2>
  {% endif %}
</body>
</html>
```

Explanation:

- **Flask Application:**
  A simple Flask application is created to serve a webpage with a form for text input.
- **API Integration:**
  Upon form submission, the Flask app sends the input text as a JSON payload to the model API using the requests library.
- **Result Display:**
  The prediction returned by the API is then rendered on the webpage.
- **Template Rendering:**
  The index.html template is used to display the form and prediction result, enabling seamless integration with the model API.

Summary Table: Integrating with Existing Systems

Aspect	Description	Tools/Technologies
API Design	Create standardized, versioned endpoints for model inference.	RESTful API, GraphQL
Microservices Architecture	Deploy model inference as independent, containerized services that can scale and be orchestrated.	Docker, Kubernetes, Docker Swarm
Data Integration	Ensure efficient storage and retrieval of model predictions.	Databases (SQL/NoSQL), Data Warehouses
Workflow Orchestration	Automate end-to-end data pipelines	Apache Airflow, Prefect

	that include model inference.	
Application Integration	Seamlessly incorporate model APIs into web applications or backend services.	Flask, Django, FastAPI, API Gateways

Deploying a fine-tuned model involves not only optimizing it for production but also integrating it seamlessly with existing systems and applications. Real-time inference and batch processing represent two different strategies for serving model predictions—each tailored to specific use cases and operational constraints. Real-time inference is ideal for interactive applications that demand low latency, while batch processing is more suited for non-interactive, high-throughput tasks.

Furthermore, effective integration requires robust API design, containerization, scalable microservices architecture, and smooth data workflows. The detailed code examples and summary tables provided in this chapter illustrate practical approaches for both serving models and integrating them into broader application ecosystems.

By following these strategies, you can ensure that your fine-tuned models are not only performant in isolation but also deliver real value when deployed as part of a complete, scalable, and maintainable production system.

Chapter 14: Ethics, Security, and Responsible AI

As large language models (LLMs) become increasingly integrated into diverse applications, it is essential to consider the ethical, security, and responsible use aspects of these models. Fine-tuning LLMs for specific tasks introduces new challenges and responsibilities, as models may inadvertently perpetuate biases, propagate misinformation, or even be misused. This chapter examines ethical considerations in fine-tuning LLMs and discusses strategies for mitigating bias and ensuring fairness in model outputs. The focus is on providing clear, practical guidance for responsible AI development.

14.1 Ethical Considerations in Fine-Tuning LLMs

Ethical considerations in fine-tuning LLMs involve understanding the potential societal impacts, identifying risks associated with model misuse, and ensuring that model development aligns with ethical principles and regulatory requirements.

Key Ethical Issues

1. **Data Privacy and Consent:**
   - **Sensitive Data:** Fine-tuning may involve using data that contains personal, confidential, or sensitive information.
   - **Consent:** It is crucial to ensure that data used for fine-tuning is collected with proper consent and complies with data protection regulations (e.g., GDPR, HIPAA).
2. **Transparency and Accountability:**
   - **Model Interpretability:** Stakeholders should be able to understand how a model reaches its decisions.
   - **Documentation:** Clear documentation (e.g., model cards, data sheets) should be provided to explain the model's training data, design choices, and limitations.
   - **Accountability:** Establish procedures for auditing and revising models if ethical issues arise.
3. **Risk of Misinformation and Harmful Outputs:**
   - **False Information:** Models may generate inaccurate or misleading content that could have serious implications, especially in sensitive domains like health or finance.
   - **Harmful Content:** There is a risk that models may produce content that is biased, discriminatory, or harmful if not properly managed.

4. **Intellectual Property:**
    - **Data Ownership:** Ensure that the data used for fine-tuning is legally obtained and that intellectual property rights are respected.
    - **Reuse of Models:** Be cautious when deploying models that have been fine-tuned on copyrighted or proprietary data.

Best Practices for Ethical Fine-Tuning

- **Data Auditing:**
  Regularly audit datasets for sensitive information and ensure that data is anonymized when necessary.
- **Bias and Fairness Assessments:**
  Evaluate models not only for performance metrics but also for fairness, checking whether the outputs disproportionately affect certain groups.
- **Transparency Documentation:**
  Publish detailed documentation that explains model decisions, data sources, and potential limitations. Tools like model cards and datasheets can be highly effective.
- **User Consent and Feedback:**
  Incorporate mechanisms for user feedback and ensure that users are informed about how their data is used.

Example: Ethical Documentation Template

Below is an example of a simple documentation template (a model card excerpt) that can be used to communicate ethical considerations:

markdown

Model Card: [Model Name]

Intended Use

- **Primary Applications:** [e.g., sentiment analysis, content summarization]

- **Out-of-Scope Applications:** [e.g., medical diagnosis, legal advice]

Data and Training

- **Data Sources:** [List of data sources and their characteristics]

- **Data Privacy:** [Explanation of anonymization and consent procedures]

- **Preprocessing Steps:** [Data cleaning, tokenization, etc.]

Ethical Considerations

- **Bias Evaluation:** [Methods used to assess bias and fairness]

- **Limitations:** [Known issues, such as potential for harmful outputs]

- **User Consent:** [Details on how user data is protected]

Responsible Deployment

- **Monitoring:** [Plans for continuous monitoring and feedback loops]

- **Mitigation Strategies:** [Approaches for handling misinformation and harmful content]

Explanation:
This template helps ensure transparency and accountability by clearly outlining how the model was built, what data was used, and how ethical considerations were addressed.

14.2 Mitigating Bias and Ensuring Fairness

Bias in language models can arise from the data used during pre-training and fine-tuning, leading to outputs that are skewed or discriminatory. Mitigating bias and ensuring fairness is critical for building responsible AI systems.

Identifying Bias

Bias detection can be approached through both quantitative and qualitative methods:

1. **Quantitative Methods:**
   - **Disaggregated Metrics:**
     Evaluate performance metrics (accuracy, precision, recall, F1-score) across different demographic groups.
   - **Bias Metrics:**
     Use statistical measures such as Statistical Parity Difference, Equal Opportunity Difference, or Disparate Impact Ratio to quantify bias.
   - **Automated Auditing Tools:**
     Leverage tools like IBM's AI Fairness 360 or Microsoft Fairlearn to assess bias in model predictions.
2. **Qualitative Methods:**
   - **Human Evaluation:**
     Experts and diverse user groups can assess model outputs for fairness and harmful content.
   - **Error Analysis:**
     Review cases where the model's performance is notably poor for certain groups to identify patterns of bias.

Strategies to Mitigate Bias

1. **Data-Level Interventions:**
   - **Diversify Training Data:**
     Ensure that the fine-tuning dataset is representative of various groups and perspectives.
   - **Data Augmentation:**
     Use techniques such as synonym replacement or back-translation to increase the diversity of the training data.
   - **Rebalancing:**
     Apply techniques like oversampling minority classes or undersampling majority classes to balance the dataset.
2. **Algorithm-Level Interventions:**
   - **Regularization and Adversarial Training:**
     Implement adversarial training strategies that penalize biased behavior, or apply regularization techniques to avoid overfitting to biased patterns.
   - **Post-Processing:**
     Adjust model outputs after inference to correct for known biases. For example, calibrating the probabilities of certain outputs based on fairness constraints.
3. **User-Centric Approaches:**
   - **Feedback Mechanisms:**
     Incorporate user feedback to continuously monitor and correct biases.

- ○ **Transparency:**
  Clearly communicate the known limitations and potential biases of the model to end users.

Example: Evaluating and Mitigating Bias with Python

Below is an example of how to evaluate bias using disaggregated metrics, followed by a simple rebalancing strategy for a classification task.

python

```python
import numpy as np

from sklearn.metrics import accuracy_score, precision_recall_fscore_support


# Simulated true labels and predictions for two demographic groups

true_labels_group1 = np.array([0, 1, 0, 1, 0])

predictions_group1 = np.array([0, 1, 1, 1, 0])


true_labels_group2 = np.array([0, 1, 0, 1, 0])

predictions_group2 = np.array([1, 1, 0, 1, 1])


def compute_group_metrics(true_labels, predictions):

    accuracy = accuracy_score(true_labels, predictions)

    precision, recall, f1, _ = precision_recall_fscore_support(true_labels, predictions, average="binary")

    return {"accuracy": accuracy, "precision": precision, "recall": recall, "f1": f1}
```

```python
metrics_group1 = compute_group_metrics(true_labels_group1,
predictions_group1)

metrics_group2 = compute_group_metrics(true_labels_group2,
predictions_group2)


print("Metrics for Group 1:", metrics_group1)

print("Metrics for Group 2:", metrics_group2)


# Simple rebalancing strategy: Oversample minority class in a dataset
(illustrative)

from imblearn.over_sampling import SMOTE

from sklearn.datasets import make_classification


# Create a sample imbalanced dataset

X, y = make_classification(n_samples=1000, n_features=20,
n_informative=2, n_redundant=10, weights=[0.9, 0.1], random_state=42)

print("Original class distribution:", np.bincount(y))


# Apply SMOTE to balance the dataset

smote = SMOTE(random_state=42)

X_resampled, y_resampled = smote.fit_resample(X, y)

print("Resampled class distribution:", np.bincount(y_resampled))
```

Explanation:

- **Group Metrics Calculation:**
  The code calculates accuracy, precision, recall, and F1-score separately for two hypothetical demographic groups, which helps identify any disparities.
- **Rebalancing with SMOTE:**
  The oversampling technique SMOTE (Synthetic Minority Over-sampling Technique) is applied to balance the class distribution in an imbalanced dataset, which is one data-level intervention to mitigate bias.

Summary Table: Mitigating Bias and Ensuring Fairness

Strategy	Description	Benefits
Data Diversification	Collect and augment diverse and representative data.	Reduces sampling bias; improves generalization.
Rebalancing Techniques	Oversample minority classes or undersample majority classes.	Mitigates class imbalance; enhances fairness.
Algorithm-Level Interventions	Implement adversarial training, regularization, or post-processing.	Directly addresses model behavior; reduces learned bias.
Human-in-the-Loop Feedback	Involve experts and end-users to review outputs and provide feedback.	Provides qualitative insights; ongoing model improvement.

Ethical considerations, fairness, and bias evaluation are critical components of responsible AI development. Fine-tuning LLMs for specific applications must be approached with a focus on minimizing unintended harm and ensuring equitable performance across diverse user groups. By integrating ethical data practices, performing rigorous bias evaluations using both quantitative and qualitative methods, and employing strategies such as data diversification, rebalancing, and adversarial training, you can significantly mitigate bias and enhance fairness.

Continuous monitoring and transparency—through detailed documentation and user feedback mechanisms—further ensure that models remain accountable and trustworthy. The comprehensive guidelines, code examples, and summary tables provided in this chapter offer a robust framework for developing and maintaining ethically sound, fair, and responsible AI systems.

14.3 Data Privacy and Security Best Practices

When fine-tuning and deploying large language models (LLMs), it is essential to prioritize data privacy and security. Handling sensitive information requires implementing robust policies and technical measures to protect data throughout the model's lifecycle—from data collection and preprocessing to training, deployment, and ongoing monitoring. This section outlines best practices to safeguard data and ensure secure operations.

Key Areas of Focus

1. **Data Collection and Storage:**
   - **Data Minimization:**
     Collect only the data necessary for the task. Avoid gathering extraneous or overly sensitive information.
   - **Encryption:**
     Encrypt data both in transit and at rest. Use protocols such as TLS for data transmission and industry-standard encryption (e.g., AES-256) for stored data.
   - **Access Control:**
     Implement strict access controls to ensure that only authorized personnel can access sensitive data. Use role-based access control (RBAC) and multi-factor authentication (MFA).
2. **Data Anonymization and Pseudonymization:**
   - **Anonymization:**
     Remove personally identifiable information (PII) from datasets to protect individual privacy. Techniques include masking, redaction, and generalization.
   - **Pseudonymization:**
     Replace sensitive identifiers with pseudonyms. While not as secure as full anonymization, it helps reduce risk if data is compromised.

3. **Secure Data Preprocessing and Model Training:**
   - **Data Auditing:**
     Regularly audit datasets to ensure compliance with privacy policies and regulatory requirements. Identify and mitigate potential data leaks.
   - **Environment Isolation:**
     Use isolated environments (e.g., virtual machines or containers) for data processing and model training. This minimizes the risk of unauthorized data access.
   - **Logging and Monitoring:**
     Maintain detailed logs of data access and modifications. Monitor for unusual activity that could indicate a breach.
4. **Model Deployment and Inference Security:**
   - **API Security:**
     When serving models via APIs, secure endpoints using authentication, authorization, and encryption. Implement rate limiting and monitoring to prevent abuse.
   - **Model Access Controls:**
     Restrict access to deployed models. Use network segmentation and firewalls to protect inference servers.
   - **Regular Security Audits:**
     Conduct periodic security audits and penetration testing to identify vulnerabilities in the deployment pipeline.

Code Example: Securing Data Transmission with TLS in a Python Server

Below is an example of configuring a simple FastAPI server to use TLS (HTTPS) for secure data transmission.

python

```python
from fastapi import FastAPI

import uvicorn


app = FastAPI()


@app.get("/")
```

```python
async def read_root():

    return {"message": "Secure API is running."}


if __name__ == "__main__":

    # Ensure you have 'cert.pem' and 'key.pem' files for TLS/SSL

    uvicorn.run(app, host="0.0.0.0", port=8000, ssl_certfile="cert.pem",
ssl_keyfile="key.pem")
```

Explanation:

- **SSL/TLS Certificates:**
  The ssl_certfile and ssl_keyfile parameters in uvicorn.run specify the certificate and private key files required to enable HTTPS.
- **Secure API:**
  This configuration ensures that all data transmitted to and from the API is encrypted, protecting it from interception.

Summary Table: Data Privacy and Security Best Practices

Area	Best Practices	Key Technologies /Methods
Data Collection	Collect minimal necessary data; use encryption and access control.	TLS, AES-256, RBAC, MFA
Data Anonymizatio n	Anonymize or pseudonymize PII; audit data regularly.	Masking, redaction, pseudonymizati on techniques

Preprocessing & Training	Use isolated environments; log and monitor data access.	Virtual machines, containers, audit logs
Deployment Security	Secure API endpoints; enforce network-level protections; conduct regular security audits.	HTTPS, firewalls, penetration testing

14.4 Transparency, Accountability, and Regulatory Compliance

Ensuring transparency, accountability, and regulatory compliance is crucial when deploying LLMs, especially given their potential impact on society. Organizations must be able to explain how their models work, the data they are trained on, and how decisions are made. This builds trust among users and helps adhere to legal and ethical standards.

Transparency

Key Elements:

1. **Model Documentation:**
   - **Model Cards:**
     Provide comprehensive documentation that details the model's intended use, training data, performance metrics, limitations, and potential biases.
   - **Datasheets for Datasets:**
     Document the provenance, composition, and preprocessing steps of datasets to provide context for the model's behavior.
2. **Explainability:**
   - **Interpretability Tools:**
     Use tools like SHAP (SHapley Additive exPlanations) or LIME (Local Interpretable Model-agnostic Explanations) to provide insights into model predictions.

- **User-Friendly Summaries:**
  Create summaries or visualizations that help non-technical stakeholders understand how the model works.

Accountability

Key Elements:

1. **Audit Trails:**
   - **Logging:**
     Maintain comprehensive logs of model training, updates, and deployment events to enable auditing.
   - **Versioning:**
     Track versions of models and datasets, so any changes can be reviewed and rolled back if necessary.
2. **Responsibility and Governance:**
   - **Ethics Committees:**
     Establish internal committees to oversee AI development and ensure adherence to ethical standards.
   - **Clear Ownership:**
     Define accountability structures for model performance and decision-making, ensuring that responsible parties can be identified.

Regulatory Compliance

Key Considerations:

1. **Legal Frameworks:**
   - **GDPR, HIPAA, CCPA, etc.:**
     Understand and comply with data protection laws relevant to the jurisdiction in which the model is deployed.
   - **Industry Standards:**
     Follow guidelines and standards specific to your industry (e.g., healthcare, finance).
2. **Risk Management:**
   - **Impact Assessments:**
     Conduct regular risk assessments and audits to evaluate the potential impacts of the model on different user groups.
   - **Mitigation Plans:**
     Develop strategies for mitigating identified risks, including procedures for addressing adverse outcomes.

Example: Creating a Model Card for Transparency

Below is an example template for a model card that outlines key transparency and accountability information.

markdown

Model Card: [Model Name]

Model Details

- **Model Architecture:** [e.g., BERT-base, GPT-2]

- **Version:** 1.0

- **Date:** YYYY-MM-DD

Intended Use

- **Primary Use Cases:** [e.g., sentiment analysis, question answering]

- **Out-of-Scope Use Cases:** [e.g., legal advice, medical diagnosis]

Training Data

- **Data Sources:** [List of datasets and their sources]

- **Preprocessing Steps:** [Data cleaning, tokenization, etc.]

- **Data Privacy:** [Description of anonymization and consent procedures]

Performance Metrics

- **Accuracy:** X%

- **F1-Score:** Y

- **Bias and Fairness:** [Results of fairness audits, disaggregated metrics]

Ethical Considerations

- **Known Limitations:** [e.g., potential biases, performance degradation on specific demographics]

- **Risk Mitigation Strategies:** [Plans for regular audits, user feedback mechanisms]

Regulatory Compliance

- **Data Protection Laws:** [Compliance with GDPR, HIPAA, etc.]

- **Audit Trail:** [Description of logging and versioning systems]

Contact Information

- **Responsible Team:** [Team or individual responsible for the model]

- **Support Email:** [Contact email for inquiries]

Explanation:

- **Comprehensive Documentation:**
  This model card covers details about the model architecture, training data, performance metrics, ethical considerations, and regulatory compliance.
- **Stakeholder Communication:**
  Provides a clear, accessible overview for both technical and non-technical stakeholders, promoting transparency and accountability.

Summary Table: Transparency, Accountability, and Regulatory Compliance

Aspect	Key Elements	Tools/Methods

Transparency	Model cards, datasheets, explainability tools.	SHAP, LIME, documentation templates.
Accountability	Audit trails, versioning, clear governance structures.	Logging systems, version control (Git, MLflow).
Regulatory Compliance	Adherence to data protection laws, risk assessments, impact assessments.	GDPR/HIPAA/ CCPA guidelines, legal audits, risk management frameworks.

Ensuring data privacy, security, transparency, accountability, and regulatory compliance is paramount in the ethical deployment of fine-tuned language models. By implementing robust data protection measures, documenting model details transparently, and establishing clear accountability structures, organizations can build trust with users and meet regulatory requirements.

The detailed practices, examples, and templates provided in this chapter offer a comprehensive guide to integrating ethical and secure practices into your AI workflows. With these best practices in place, you can develop and deploy language models that are not only effective but also responsible and compliant with both ethical standards and legal regulations.

Chapter 15: Case Studies and Real-World Applications

In this chapter, we explore practical examples and real-world applications of fine-tuning large language models across various industries. We examine industry-specific solutions for sectors such as legal, medical, and finance, and then review success stories and lessons learned from deployments in real-world environments. These case studies highlight both the transformative potential and the challenges of adapting language models to specialized tasks.

15.1 Fine-Tuning for Industry-Specific Solutions (Legal, Medical, Finance)

Fine-tuning language models for industry-specific applications involves tailoring a pre-trained model to meet the unique vocabulary, context, and regulatory requirements of a particular domain. Below are detailed overviews of how fine-tuning has been applied in three critical sectors.

Legal Sector

Challenges:

- **Complex Terminology:** Legal language includes complex terms, phrases, and citations that are uncommon in general corpora.
- **Document Variety:** Legal documents range from contracts and briefs to opinions and case law, each requiring specialized handling.
- **Regulatory and Ethical Concerns:** Accuracy is paramount due to potential legal liabilities and the need for strict confidentiality.

Fine-Tuning Approach:

- **Domain-Specific Datasets:** Curate corpora comprising court opinions, legal briefs, contracts, and statutes.
- **Custom Tokenization:** Adapt tokenizers to include legal jargon and citations.
- **Model Adaptation:** Fine-tune models like BERT or GPT on legal text, often with additional layers (e.g., adapter modules) to capture domain nuances.
- **Evaluation:** Use metrics such as precision and recall for tasks like document classification and named entity recognition, along with qualitative reviews by legal experts.

Example Code Snippet: Fine-Tuning on Legal Data

python

```python
from transformers import AutoTokenizer,
AutoModelForSequenceClassification, Trainer, TrainingArguments

from datasets import load_dataset


# Load a pre-trained model and tokenizer for legal document classification

model_name = "bert-base-uncased"

tokenizer = AutoTokenizer.from_pretrained(model_name)

model =
AutoModelForSequenceClassification.from_pretrained(model_name,
num_labels=3)  # e.g., contract, brief, opinion


# Assume a legal dataset is available in Hugging Face format

legal_dataset = load_dataset("your_legal_dataset")  # Placeholder dataset
name


# Tokenization function tailored for legal text

def tokenize_legal_text(examples):

    return tokenizer(examples["text"], padding="max_length",
truncation=True, max_length=256)


tokenized_dataset = legal_dataset.map(tokenize_legal_text,
batched=True)
```

```python
# Define training arguments for fine-tuning

training_args = TrainingArguments(

    output_dir="./legal_finetuned_model",

    num_train_epochs=4,

    per_device_train_batch_size=16,

    per_device_eval_batch_size=16,

    evaluation_strategy="epoch",

    learning_rate=2e-5,

    weight_decay=0.01,

)


# Initialize Trainer and start fine-tuning

trainer = Trainer(

    model=model,

    args=training_args,

    train_dataset=tokenized_dataset["train"],

    eval_dataset=tokenized_dataset["validation"],

)

trainer.train()
```

Medical Sector

Challenges:

- **Specialized Medical Terminology:** Fine-tuning requires handling clinical language, medical abbreviations, and scientific literature.

- **Data Privacy:** Strict regulations (e.g., HIPAA) govern the use of patient data, necessitating anonymization and secure handling.
- **Critical Decision-Making:** Medical applications demand high accuracy as errors can directly impact patient care.

Fine-Tuning Approach:

- **Curated Medical Datasets:** Use datasets from medical journals, clinical records (with proper anonymization), and research publications.
- **Domain Adaptation:** Fine-tune models with techniques like intermediate fine-tuning—first on general medical literature and then on task-specific datasets (e.g., diagnosis prediction or clinical note summarization).
- **Ethical Oversight:** Implement rigorous validation with medical experts to assess model reliability.

Evaluation Metrics:

- Use clinical metrics such as sensitivity and specificity, in addition to standard metrics like F1-score.

Finance Sector

Challenges:

- **Market-Specific Language:** Financial texts include unique jargon, acronyms, and quantitative data.
- **Time-Sensitivity:** Financial decisions often require real-time analysis and predictions.
- **Risk Management:** Accuracy is critical in financial forecasting and risk assessment to avoid substantial monetary losses.

Fine-Tuning Approach:

- **Financial Datasets:** Utilize news articles, earnings reports, market data, and financial statements.
- **Sentiment and Trend Analysis:** Fine-tune models for tasks such as market sentiment analysis, fraud detection, and automated report generation.
- **Integration with Quantitative Models:** Combine textual analysis with quantitative financial models for improved decision-making.

Evaluation Metrics:

- Evaluate using metrics like accuracy, F1-score, and domain-specific KPIs (e.g., prediction accuracy of market trends).

Summary Table: Industry-Specific Fine-Tuning

Industry	Key Challenges	Fine-Tuning Approach	Evaluation Metrics
Legal	Complex terminology, diverse document types, regulatory concerns	Use legal corpora, custom tokenization, domain-specific model adaptation	Precision, recall, F1, expert qualitative review
Medical	Specialized language, data privacy, high-stakes decisions	Anonymized medical datasets, intermediate fine-tuning, expert validation	Sensitivity, specificity, F1, clinical accuracy
Finance	Market-specific language, time-sensitivity, risk management	Financial datasets, sentiment analysis, integration with quantitative models	Accuracy, F1, domain-specific KPIs, trend prediction accuracy

15.2 Success Stories and Lessons Learned

Real-world implementations of fine-tuning strategies provide valuable insights into both the potential benefits and the challenges of deploying large language models. This section highlights several success stories and summarizes the key lessons learned from these deployments.

Success Story 1: Customer Support Chatbot

Background:
A multinational company deployed a fine-tuned language model as the backbone of its customer support chatbot. The model was fine-tuned on a diverse dataset of customer interactions and support tickets.

Key Achievements:

- **Improved Response Accuracy:**
  The chatbot achieved a significant reduction in misclassified queries, improving overall customer satisfaction.
- **Faster Response Times:**
  Real-time inference capabilities allowed for instant responses, enhancing user experience.
- **Scalability:**
  The solution scaled efficiently across multiple regions with varying customer volumes.

Lessons Learned:

- **Continuous Feedback:**
  Regular updates based on user feedback were crucial for maintaining performance.
- **Robust Monitoring:**
  Implementing continuous monitoring helped quickly identify and rectify any performance issues.
- **Hybrid Fine-Tuning:**
  Combining supervised fine-tuning with reinforcement learning from human feedback further refined the model's outputs.

Success Story 2: Legal Document Analysis Tool

Background:
A legal tech firm fine-tuned a language model on a large corpus of legal documents to automate the classification and summarization of contracts and legal briefs.

Key Achievements:

- **High Accuracy:**
  The tool achieved state-of-the-art accuracy in categorizing legal documents, reducing manual review time.
- **Efficiency Gains:**
  Automated summarization helped legal professionals quickly extract key information from lengthy documents.
- **User Trust:**
  Transparent documentation and expert oversight enhanced user trust in the tool's outputs.

Lessons Learned:

- **Domain-Specific Training:**
  Customizing the model with domain-specific data is critical for achieving high accuracy.
- **Ethical and Regulatory Compliance:**
  Adherence to legal and ethical standards was essential, given the sensitive nature of legal data.
- **Scalable Infrastructure:**
  Investing in robust cloud infrastructure enabled the tool to handle large volumes of documents efficiently.

Success Story 3: Financial Market Sentiment Analysis

Background:
A financial services firm fine-tuned a transformer-based model for market sentiment analysis by leveraging news articles, social media feeds, and financial reports.

Key Achievements:

- **Real-Time Insights:**
  The model provided real-time sentiment analysis that informed trading strategies.
- **Cost Savings:**
  Parameter-efficient fine-tuning methods minimized computational costs while maintaining high performance.
- **Strategic Advantage:**
  The insights generated by the model gave the firm a competitive edge in rapidly evolving markets.

Lessons Learned:

- **Integration with Quantitative Models:**
  Combining qualitative sentiment analysis with quantitative financial models resulted in more robust predictions.
- **Data Quality:**
  Ensuring high-quality, up-to-date data was critical to the model's success.
- **Flexibility:**
  The ability to quickly update and fine-tune the model as new data emerged was key to maintaining accuracy over time.

Summary Table: Success Stories and Lessons Learned

Success Story	Key Achievements	Lessons Learned
Customer Support Chatbot	Reduced misclassification, real-time responses, scalable across regions	Importance of continuous feedback, robust monitoring, and hybrid fine-tuning strategies
Legal Document Analysis Tool	High accuracy in classification and summarization, efficiency gains, increased trust	Need for domain-specific training, regulatory compliance, and scalable infrastructure
Financial Market Sentiment Analysis	Real-time sentiment insights, cost savings, strategic competitive advantage	Integration with quantitative models, maintaining high-quality data, flexibility in updates

Real-world case studies provide compelling evidence of the transformative potential of fine-tuning large language models for industry-specific applications. From customer support to legal analysis and financial sentiment tracking, these success stories demonstrate that, with careful data curation, domain-specific adaptation, and robust deployment strategies, LLMs can deliver significant value.

At the same time, the lessons learned underscore the importance of continuous monitoring, ethical considerations, and infrastructure scalability. By combining these insights with the technical strategies outlined in earlier chapters, practitioners can develop and deploy fine-tuned models that are not only highly effective but also adaptable to the evolving needs of diverse industries.

15.3 Collaborative Projects and Open-Source Contributions

Collaborative projects and open-source contributions have played a pivotal role in the rapid advancement of fine-tuning techniques for large language models (LLMs). By pooling resources, expertise, and data, communities and organizations accelerate research, standardize best practices, and drive innovation in AI. In this section, we discuss the benefits of collaborative projects, highlight notable open-source initiatives, and provide guidance on how to contribute and leverage these resources in your own projects.

The Importance of Collaboration in AI

- **Accelerated Innovation:**
  Collaboration brings together diverse expertise from academia, industry, and independent developers. This diversity fosters innovation, leading to faster advancements in model architectures, training techniques, and evaluation methods.
- **Resource Sharing:**
  Open-source projects enable sharing of data, code, and pre-trained models, lowering the barriers to entry for individuals and organizations. This is particularly valuable in fine-tuning, where large datasets and significant computational resources are often required.
- **Standardization of Best Practices:**
  Collaborative efforts lead to the development of standardized benchmarks, evaluation metrics, and reproducibility protocols, ensuring that improvements are well documented and comparable across projects.
- **Community Support and Feedback:**
  Open-source communities provide forums for discussion, troubleshooting, and feedback. This support system is invaluable for refining fine-tuning techniques and addressing challenges in model deployment.

Notable Collaborative Projects

Several projects and repositories have emerged as central hubs for collaborative work in fine-tuning LLMs:

- **Hugging Face Transformers:**
  The Hugging Face Transformers library is one of the most prominent examples, hosting thousands of pre-trained models and enabling fine-tuning with minimal code. Its active community contributes improvements, bug fixes, and new features continuously.
- **OpenAI's GPT Series:**
  OpenAI has published multiple iterations of GPT models, which have inspired numerous research projects and open-source contributions that explore fine-tuning strategies, ethical implications, and novel applications.
- **BigScience Workshop:**
  An international collaborative effort that aims to build a large, open, multilingual language model. The project involves researchers from various countries sharing data, resources, and expertise to democratize LLM research.
- **MLPerf:**
  A collaborative benchmark suite that sets performance standards for machine learning, including fine-tuning and inference tasks. Contributions to MLPerf help standardize evaluations across diverse hardware and software configurations.

How to Contribute and Leverage Open-Source Resources

1. **Joining Communities:**
   Engage with communities on GitHub, Hugging Face forums, and specialized Slack or Discord channels. Participate in discussions, ask questions, and share your experiences.
2. **Contributing Code and Documentation:**
   Contribute improvements, new features, or bug fixes to popular repositories like Hugging Face Transformers. Good documentation and tutorials are equally valuable and help others adopt best practices.
3. **Sharing Datasets:**
   If you work with unique domain-specific datasets, consider contributing them to open repositories (ensuring that privacy and licensing requirements are met). This enriches the pool of resources available for fine-tuning.
4. **Collaborative Research:**
   Publish your findings in open-access journals or on platforms like arXiv, and share your code via repositories. Collaboration can also involve participating in challenges or competitions that promote reproducible research.

Example: Contributing to an Open-Source Project

Below is an illustrative example of how to contribute to an open-source project like the Hugging Face Transformers library.

1. **Fork the Repository:**
   Navigate to the Hugging Face Transformers GitHub page and fork the repository to your GitHub account.

Clone the Repository Locally:
bash

```
git clone https://github.com/your-username/transformers.git

cd transformers
```

Create a New Branch for Your Feature or Fix:
bash

```
git checkout -b feature/my-fine-tuning-improvement
```

2. **Implement Your Changes:**
   Edit the code or documentation as needed. For example, you might add a new function that improves the tokenization process for a specific domain.

Run Tests and Linting:
Ensure that your changes pass all existing tests and follow the repository's coding standards.
bash

```
pytest  # Run tests

flake8  # Check for linting errors
```

Commit and Push Your Changes:
bash

```
git add .
```

```
git commit -m "Improved fine-tuning tokenization for domain-specific
data"

git push origin feature/my-fine-tuning-improvement
```

3. **Open a Pull Request:**
   Submit a pull request (PR) from your branch to the main repository. Provide a clear description of your changes and the problem they address.

15.4 Future Trends and Innovation in Fine-Tuning

The field of fine-tuning LLMs is evolving rapidly, with ongoing research and emerging trends poised to shape the next generation of AI applications. In this section, we discuss future trends and innovations that are expected to influence fine-tuning strategies, model performance, and practical deployments.

Emerging Trends in Fine-Tuning

1. **Parameter-Efficient Fine-Tuning Methods:**
   Techniques like Low-Rank Adaptation (LoRA), adapter modules, and prompt tuning are expected to continue gaining traction. These methods allow for fine-tuning with significantly reduced computational resources, making it feasible to adapt massive models even in resource-constrained settings.
2. **Hybrid Training Approaches:**
   Combining supervised fine-tuning with reinforcement learning from human feedback (RLHF) or unsupervised objectives may yield models that are not only accurate but also better aligned with human values and preferences.
3. **Multi-Task and Multi-Domain Models:**
   The trend toward building models that can handle multiple tasks or domains with minimal reconfiguration is likely to grow. Future research may focus on developing models with dynamic architectures that can adapt on the fly based on the input context.
4. **Automated and Self-Supervised Fine-Tuning:**
   Advances in self-supervised learning and automated machine learning (AutoML) may lead to systems that can continuously fine-tune themselves based on new data, reducing the need for manual intervention and ensuring that models remain up-to-date with evolving information.

5. **Robustness and Fairness Enhancements:**
   Ongoing research will likely focus on building models that are more robust to adversarial inputs, exhibit fewer biases, and are fair across different demographic groups. This involves integrating ethical considerations directly into the fine-tuning process.

6. **Edge and On-Device Fine-Tuning:**
   With the growing need for real-time, low-latency applications, future trends may include techniques for fine-tuning and deploying models directly on edge devices, balancing performance with computational constraints.

Innovations in Infrastructure and Tools

1. **Enhanced Distributed Training Frameworks:**
   New frameworks and improvements in distributed training (e.g., more efficient gradient synchronization, better support for heterogeneous hardware) will enable faster fine-tuning of larger models.

2. **Integration of AI with DevOps (MLOps):**
   The rise of MLOps practices will streamline the entire lifecycle of model development—from training and fine-tuning to deployment and monitoring. Automated pipelines, continuous integration, and robust logging systems will become standard in AI workflows.

3. **Explainability and Interpretability Tools:**
   Innovations in explainability tools (such as improved SHAP or LIME implementations) will allow practitioners to better understand model decisions, identify potential biases, and improve overall transparency.

4. **Open-Source Ecosystem Expansion:**
   The open-source community will continue to grow, contributing new libraries, models, and datasets that further democratize access to state-of-the-art fine-tuning techniques.

Future Directions for Research and Development

- **Energy Efficiency:**
  With the increasing computational cost of training LLMs, future research will likely emphasize energy-efficient training and inference methods, potentially integrating hardware advancements with novel software algorithms.

- **Personalized Models:**
  As fine-tuning becomes more efficient, there may be a shift toward personalized models that are fine-tuned on individual user data, improving user experiences in applications like personal assistants and recommendation systems.

- **Regulatory and Ethical Innovations:**
  As regulations around AI and data privacy evolve, innovations in fine-tuning will

need to address these concerns proactively, integrating ethical guidelines and compliance measures into the core of model development.

Summary Table: Future Trends and Innovations in Fine-Tuning

Trend/Innovation	Description	Potential Impact
Parameter-Efficient Methods	Techniques like LoRA, adapters, and prompt tuning to reduce computational cost during fine-tuning.	More accessible fine-tuning of large models, reduced resource consumption.
Hybrid Training Approaches	Combining supervised learning, RLHF, and unsupervised objectives for balanced model alignment.	Improved alignment with human values and more robust models.
Multi-Task/Multi-Domain Models	Developing models that can adapt to multiple tasks or domains with minimal reconfiguration.	Enhanced versatility and better generalization across applications.
Automated Fine-Tuning	Self-supervised and AutoML techniques that allow continuous model updates with	Reduced manual workload, models remain

	minimal manual intervention.	current with new data.
Edge and On-Device Fine-Tuning	Techniques for fine-tuning models directly on edge devices for low-latency, real-time applications.	Improved real-time performance, broader deployment in resource-constrained environments.
Enhanced Distributed Training & MLOps	Advances in distributed training frameworks and integration of AI with DevOps practices.	Streamlined workflows, faster training cycles, and better reproducibility.
Explainability Tools	Improved interpretability methods to understand model behavior and address biases.	Increased transparency, improved trust and accountability.
Energy Efficiency and Personalizati on	Innovations to reduce energy consumption and tailor models to individual users.	Sustainable AI practices, enhanced user experiences through personalization.

Collaborative projects and open-source contributions continue to shape the landscape of fine-tuning large language models, driving innovation and accessibility. Looking forward, emerging trends such as parameter-efficient fine-tuning methods, hybrid training approaches, multi-task/multi-domain adaptation, and automated fine-tuning are set to revolutionize how models are optimized and deployed. Concurrently, advances in infrastructure, MLOps practices, and explainability tools will support the development of robust, ethical, and energy-efficient models.

By staying engaged with the open-source community and keeping abreast of future trends, practitioners can leverage these innovations to develop next-generation AI systems that are not only highly effective but also transparent, accountable, and adaptable to the ever-evolving needs of society.

Chapter 16: Future Directions and Conclusion

As the field of large language models (LLMs) continues to evolve at a rapid pace, so too do the techniques and technologies for fine-tuning them. In this concluding chapter, we explore emerging research and next-generation techniques that are set to further transform the landscape of fine-tuning, as well as outline a roadmap for continuous learning and adaptation in production environments. These discussions provide both a glimpse into the future of fine-tuning and practical guidelines for ensuring that models remain current, efficient, and aligned with evolving needs.

16.1 Emerging Research and Next-Generation Techniques

Emerging research in the field of fine-tuning is focusing on several key areas that promise to improve the performance, efficiency, and adaptability of LLMs. Here are some of the most notable trends and innovations:

Parameter-Efficient Adaptation

Researchers are developing even more efficient techniques than current methods such as LoRA, adapter modules, and prompt tuning. These approaches aim to minimize the number of trainable parameters while maintaining or improving model performance. Innovations in this area include:

- **Dynamic Parameterization:**
  Instead of using fixed low-rank approximations, dynamic parameterization techniques allow models to adjust the degree of adaptation based on the complexity of the task.
- **Meta-Learning Approaches:**
  Meta-learning (or "learning to learn") enables models to rapidly adapt to new tasks with few examples by leveraging prior fine-tuning experiences.

Hybrid Training Methods

Next-generation techniques are increasingly exploring the synergy between different training paradigms to create more robust and adaptable models:

- **Hybrid Supervised and Reinforcement Learning:**
  Combining traditional supervised fine-tuning with reinforcement learning from human feedback (RLHF) can yield models that not only achieve high accuracy on

standard benchmarks but also align more closely with human expectations and ethical standards.

- **Self-Supervised Fine-Tuning:**
  Advances in self-supervised learning are paving the way for models that continuously refine themselves using unlabeled data. This can be particularly useful in domains where labeled data is scarce or expensive to obtain.

Multi-Task and Multi-Domain Adaptation

The future of fine-tuning lies in building models that can handle a variety of tasks and domains simultaneously:

- **Unified Architectures:**
  Researchers are investigating architectures that can seamlessly switch between tasks or domains, often using shared encoders with task-specific adapters or prompt tuning techniques.
- **Continual Learning:**
  Incorporating continual learning strategies enables models to learn incrementally from streaming data without suffering from catastrophic forgetting, ensuring that models remain up-to-date as new information becomes available.

Improved Explainability and Interpretability

As fine-tuned models become more complex, understanding their decisions becomes even more critical:

- **Explainable AI (XAI) Techniques:**
  Innovations in XAI are making it possible to interpret fine-tuned model decisions, providing insights into which features or tokens influenced a particular output. Methods such as integrated gradients, SHAP, and LIME are being further refined for LLMs.
- **Transparent Fine-Tuning Processes:**
  Efforts to standardize documentation (e.g., model cards and datasheets) and logging during fine-tuning are increasing, ensuring that all stakeholders have access to comprehensive information about model behavior and decision-making processes.

Table: Emerging Research Trends in Fine-Tuning

Research Area	Key Innovations	Potential Impact

Parameter-Efficient Adaptation	Dynamic parameterization, meta-learning approaches	Further reduce resource requirements while enhancing adaptability.
Hybrid Training Methods	Combining supervised, reinforcement, and self-supervised learning	Achieve robust performance and better alignment with human values.
Multi-Task/Multi-Domain Adaptation	Unified architectures, continual learning strategies	Enable a single model to effectively handle diverse tasks and evolving data.
Improved Explainability	Advanced XAI techniques, standardized documentation practices	Enhance transparency and trust in model decisions.

16.2 Roadmap for Continuous Learning and Adaptation

To maintain the relevance and performance of fine-tuned models, organizations need to adopt a continuous learning mindset. A well-structured roadmap for continuous learning and adaptation ensures that models remain effective as data, requirements, and external conditions evolve.

Key Components of a Continuous Learning Roadmap

    1. **Automated Data Ingestion and Monitoring:**

- **Data Pipelines:**
  Develop robust pipelines for continuous data ingestion from various sources (e.g., user interactions, external feeds, sensor data). Ensure that data is cleaned, anonymized, and preprocessed consistently.
- **Performance Monitoring:**
  Implement monitoring systems that continuously track model performance metrics (accuracy, latency, bias metrics) in production. Use dashboards (e.g., Grafana, Weights & Biases) to visualize trends and detect anomalies.

2. **Scheduled Model Updates and Retraining:**
   - **Incremental Updates:**
     Establish a schedule for regular fine-tuning or retraining sessions. This could be based on time intervals (e.g., weekly, monthly) or triggered by performance thresholds.
   - **A/B Testing:**
     Use A/B testing frameworks to compare the performance of updated models against current deployments, ensuring that updates lead to real improvements before full-scale rollout.

3. **Feedback Loops and Human-in-the-Loop (HITL):**
   - **User Feedback:**
     Integrate mechanisms for collecting user feedback on model outputs, which can inform subsequent training rounds. This can be achieved through surveys, rating systems, or direct interactions.
   - **Expert Review:**
     In critical domains, involve domain experts to review and annotate model outputs periodically. Their insights can guide adjustments in fine-tuning strategies.

4. **Version Control and Experiment Tracking:**
   - **Model Versioning:**
     Utilize tools like MLflow or DVC (Data Version Control) to track changes in model architectures, hyperparameters, and training data. This ensures reproducibility and accountability.
   - **Experiment Logging:**
     Maintain detailed logs of experiments, including configuration settings and performance outcomes. Automated experiment tracking systems help identify which changes yield the best improvements.

5. **Scalable Infrastructure for Continuous Learning:**
   - **Cloud and Distributed Systems:**
     Leverage cloud platforms and distributed training frameworks to scale continuous learning operations. Containerization and orchestration tools

(e.g., Docker, Kubernetes) facilitate smooth updates and scalable deployments.

- ○ **Resource Optimization:**
  Implement strategies such as mixed-precision training and dynamic resource allocation to optimize computational costs during continuous learning cycles.

Example: Setting Up a Continuous Learning Pipeline with MLflow

Below is an illustrative example of integrating MLflow for experiment tracking during continuous learning:

python

```python
import mlflow

from transformers import AutoModelForSequenceClassification, AutoTokenizer, Trainer, TrainingArguments

from datasets import load_dataset


# Initialize MLflow experiment

mlflow.set_experiment("continuous_learning_experiment")


def train_and_log(hyperparameters):
    with mlflow.start_run():

        # Log hyperparameters

        mlflow.log_params(hyperparameters)


        # Load model and tokenizer

        model_name = hyperparameters["model_name"]
```

```python
model =
AutoModelForSequenceClassification.from_pretrained(model_name,
num_labels=2)

tokenizer = AutoTokenizer.from_pretrained(model_name)


# Load dataset (e.g., IMDB dataset)

dataset = load_dataset("imdb")

train_dataset = dataset["train"].shuffle(seed=42).select(range(2000))

val_dataset = dataset["test"].shuffle(seed=42).select(range(500))


def tokenize_function(examples):

    return tokenizer(examples["text"], padding="max_length",
truncation=True, max_length=128)


train_dataset = train_dataset.map(tokenize_function, batched=True)

val_dataset = val_dataset.map(tokenize_function, batched=True)


# Define training arguments

training_args = TrainingArguments(

    output_dir="./results",

    num_train_epochs=hyperparameters["epochs"],

    per_device_train_batch_size=hyperparameters["batch_size"],

    per_device_eval_batch_size=hyperparameters["batch_size"],

    learning_rate=hyperparameters["learning_rate"],

    evaluation_strategy="epoch",
```

```python
        logging_steps=50,
    )

    trainer = Trainer(
        model=model,
        args=training_args,
        train_dataset=train_dataset,
        eval_dataset=val_dataset,
    )

    trainer.train()
    eval_results = trainer.evaluate()

    # Log evaluation metrics
    mlflow.log_metrics(eval_results)
    return eval_results

# Example hyperparameters for one training cycle
hyperparameters = {
    "model_name": "bert-base-uncased",
    "epochs": 3,
    "batch_size": 16,
    "learning_rate": 2e-5
```

```
}

results = train_and_log(hyperparameters)

print("Evaluation Results:", results)
```

Explanation:

- **MLflow Integration:**
  The code demonstrates how to use MLflow to track hyperparameters, training metrics, and evaluation outcomes.
- **Continuous Learning Cycle:**
  The function train_and_log encapsulates one training cycle, allowing the experiment to be repeated with different hyperparameters as new data becomes available.
- **Experiment Logging:**
  MLflow records the results of each cycle, facilitating comparison and ensuring reproducibility.

Summary Table: Roadmap for Continuous Learning and Adaptation

Component	Description	Tools/Methods
Automated Data Ingestion & Monitoring	Continuous collection of new data and monitoring of performance metrics in production.	Data pipelines, dashboards (Grafana, W&B), logging systems
Scheduled Model Updates	Regular retraining or fine-tuning sessions based on time intervals	Cron jobs, A/B testing frameworks,

	or performance triggers.	automated retraining scripts
Feedback Loops & HITL	Incorporate user and expert feedback to guide model improvements.	Surveys, rating systems, expert reviews
Version Control & Experiment Tracking	Track model versions and training experiments to ensure reproducibility and accountability.	MLflow, DVC, Git
Scalable Infrastructure	Utilize cloud and distributed systems to support continuous learning operations.	Docker, Kubernetes, cloud GPU clusters

The future of fine-tuning and deploying large language models hinges on continuous learning and adaptation. Emerging research and next-generation techniques promise to make fine-tuning more efficient, adaptable, and aligned with human values. At the same time, establishing a robust roadmap for continuous learning—encompassing automated data ingestion, regular model updates, feedback loops, experiment tracking, and scalable infrastructure—is essential for maintaining model performance over time.

By adopting these strategies, organizations can ensure that their models remain state-of-the-art and responsive to new data, user feedback, and evolving requirements. The detailed explanations, code examples, and summary tables provided in this chapter offer a comprehensive guide for implementing continuous learning pipelines that drive ongoing improvements and sustain high levels of performance in real-world applications.

16.3 Building a Community of Practice

Building a community of practice is essential for advancing the field of fine-tuning large language models and artificial intelligence in general. A community of practice brings together practitioners, researchers, and enthusiasts to share insights, solve problems collaboratively, and collectively drive innovation. In this section, we discuss the importance of such communities, strategies for establishing and nurturing them, and practical tips for leveraging collaborative efforts to improve both individual skills and the overall state of the art.

Why Build a Community of Practice?

- **Shared Knowledge and Best Practices:**
  A community of practice enables members to exchange insights, tools, and techniques that have proven effective in real-world scenarios. This collaborative learning environment accelerates the dissemination of best practices in model fine-tuning, deployment, and monitoring.
- **Collaboration and Innovation:**
  Working together encourages the development of novel ideas and interdisciplinary solutions. By pooling expertise from various domains—such as computer science, statistics, ethics, and domain-specific knowledge—communities can address complex challenges more effectively.
- **Professional Growth and Networking:**
  Participation in a community provides opportunities for mentorship, networking, and career development. It creates a platform for practitioners to showcase their work, collaborate on projects, and stay updated with emerging trends and research.
- **Resource Sharing:**
  Communities can collectively build repositories of datasets, code libraries, documentation, and tutorials. This shared resource pool lowers the barrier to entry for newcomers and enhances the overall quality of work within the field.

Strategies for Establishing a Community of Practice

1. **Leverage Online Platforms:**
   Utilize platforms such as GitHub, Slack, Discord, and specialized forums (e.g., Hugging Face forums, AI Stack Exchange) to create spaces for discussion and collaboration. For example, GitHub repositories with open issues and pull requests can serve as hubs for sharing code and feedback.
2. **Organize Regular Meetings and Workshops:**
   Host webinars, virtual meetups, hackathons, or local meetups to discuss recent

advancements, challenges, and best practices in fine-tuning and model deployment. Regular events help keep the community active and engaged.

3. **Create and Maintain Documentation:**
   Develop comprehensive guides, blog posts, and video tutorials on fine-tuning techniques, evaluation methods, and deployment strategies. Open-source projects and collaborative documents (e.g., shared Google Docs or a community wiki) can serve as living resources.

4. **Encourage Open-Source Contributions:**
   Promote collaborative projects where members can contribute code, datasets, and research papers. Initiatives like the Hugging Face Transformers library have shown the power of collective development in rapidly advancing the field.

5. **Establish Mentorship Programs:**
   Pair experienced practitioners with newcomers to facilitate knowledge transfer. Mentorship can help newcomers navigate complex topics, adopt best practices, and integrate more effectively into the community.

6. **Foster Inclusivity and Diversity:**
   Ensure that the community is welcoming to people from various backgrounds, disciplines, and geographic locations. Diverse perspectives enrich discussions and drive more innovative solutions.

Example: Community Engagement Initiative

Imagine launching a "Fine-Tuning Fridays" series—a weekly online meeting where community members present short talks on their latest projects, share challenges, and discuss emerging trends. These sessions can be recorded and shared on platforms like YouTube or a community website to broaden the reach and impact.

Summary Table: Key Elements of a Community of Practice

Element	Description	Examples/Tools
Knowledge Sharing	Exchange of best practices, research findings, and case studies.	GitHub repositories, blogs, webinars.

Collaboration	Joint projects and problem-solving initiatives.	Hackathons, open-source contributions, joint research papers.
Networking	Opportunities for mentorship, career development, and professional growth.	Online forums, Slack/Discord channels, LinkedIn groups.
Resource Pooling	Shared datasets, code libraries, tutorials, and documentation.	Community wikis, open-source repositories.
Inclusivity	Encouraging diverse participation and equitable access to resources.	Diversity initiatives, mentorship programs, community guidelines.

16.4 Final Thoughts and Encouragement for Practitioners

As we conclude this exploration of fine-tuning large language models, it is important to reflect on the journey, acknowledge the challenges, and embrace the opportunities ahead. The rapid evolution of AI offers both immense potential and significant responsibilities. Here are some final thoughts and words of encouragement for practitioners embarking on or continuing their work in this exciting field.

Embrace Lifelong Learning

- **Continuous Skill Development:**
  The field of AI, particularly fine-tuning and deploying LLMs, is dynamic and fast-paced. Stay curious and continually update your skills by engaging with the latest research, attending conferences, and participating in online courses.

- **Experiment and Innovate:**
  Don't be afraid to experiment with new techniques or to combine different methods in creative ways. Innovation often arises from trying unconventional approaches and learning from failures.

Cultivate a Collaborative Mindset

- **Share Your Knowledge:**
  Whether through writing blog posts, contributing to open-source projects, or mentoring others, sharing your experiences enriches the community and accelerates collective progress.
- **Seek Feedback and Collaboration:**
  Collaboration is key to overcoming challenges. Engage with peers, seek constructive feedback, and work together on solving complex problems. Remember, no one has all the answers, and collective wisdom is a powerful asset.

Stay Ethical and Responsible

- **Prioritize Ethics:**
  As you work on fine-tuning and deploying language models, always keep ethical considerations at the forefront. Ensure that your models are fair, transparent, and secure, and that they adhere to both legal regulations and societal values.
- **Be Accountable:**
  Document your work, track your experiments, and be transparent about the limitations of your models. Accountability builds trust with users and stakeholders and is essential for responsible AI development.

Look to the Future with Optimism

- **Emerging Opportunities:**
  The future of fine-tuning is filled with exciting possibilities—from parameter-efficient methods to hybrid training approaches and automated continuous learning systems. These innovations will not only enhance model performance but also make advanced AI more accessible.
- **Community and Collaboration:**
  The AI community is vibrant, innovative, and supportive. By building a community of practice, you can contribute to and benefit from collective advancements that shape the future of AI.

Final Words of Encouragement

As you continue your journey in fine-tuning large language models, remember that every challenge is an opportunity to learn and grow. The skills you develop and the collaborations you forge will not only advance your own work but also contribute to the broader field of AI. Stay resilient, remain curious, and keep pushing the boundaries of what is possible. Your efforts today will pave the way for the next generation of AI applications that are more efficient, ethical, and impactful.

In this final chapter, we have explored emerging research trends, outlined a roadmap for continuous learning and adaptation, discussed the importance of building a community of practice, and offered final thoughts to inspire practitioners. The future of fine-tuning is bright, with groundbreaking techniques and collaborative initiatives continually pushing the field forward. As you apply these insights and strategies in your own work, you play a vital role in shaping the future of AI—one that is innovative, responsible, and inclusive.

Keep learning, keep sharing, and above all, remain committed to the ethical development and deployment of technology that benefits all of society.